CONVERTED SPACES
CONVERTIR L'ESPACE
VERWANDELTE RÄUME

CONVERTED SPACES
CONVERTIR L'ESPACE
VERWANDELTE RÄUME

ELERGREEN

EVERGREEN is an imprint of
Taschen GmbH

© 2006 TASCHEN GmbH

Hohenzollernring 53, D-50672 Köln

www.taschen.com

Editor Editrice Redakteur:
Simone Schleifer

Editorial assistant Assistant d'édition Verlagsassistentin:
Cinta Martí

English translation Traduction anglaise Englische Übersetzung:
Jane Wintle

French translation Traduction française Französische Übersetzung:
Marion Westerhoff

German translation Traduction allemande Deutsche Übersetzung:
Susanne Engler

Proof reading Relecture Korrektur:
Matthew Clarke, Marie-Pierre Santamarina, Martin Rolshoven

Art director Direction artistique Art Direktor:
Mireia Casanovas Soley

Graphic design and layout Mise en page et maquette Graphische Gestaltung und Layout:
Elisabet Rodríguez

Printed by Imprimé par Gedruckt durch:
Gráficas Toledo, Spain

ISBN: 3-8228-5147-7

Contents Index Inhalt

The task of restoring a building can sometimes prove more difficult than constructing a new one from scratch, not only because some parts of it may have to be preserved on account of their historical value, but also because it is unusual to have certain knowledge of the state of its structure before embarking on the project. These problems aside, drawing up an action plan for the conversion of a building poses a challenge to any architect, as it requires strategies very different from those developed for empty lots.

There are a host of reasons why buildings are converted instead of making way for a new one. In most cases, however, the determining factors are construction regulations that prevent it from being demolished, the financial advantages of making use of an existing structure, or the owners' desire to live in a home that preserves its period charm while benefiting from modern conveniences. Whatever the reason, a project has to start from these premises, while also fulfilling the expectations of its future occupants and their lifestyle.

The European tendency to respect the buildings of the past in the aftermath of World War II has led, in recent years, to a certain degree of artificiality, and many projects have fallen back on ill-informed traditionalism or on so-called restorations that only preserve a building's façade but are otherwise entirely new. Such practices have been counteracted by the emergence of a more enlightened approach that considers refurbishment as the adaptation of an old building to contemporary requirements and places less emphasis on a dialogue with the past. Although this approach may seem somewhat overbearing, a clear, decisive intervention with modern materials is often more respectful than others that, behind a supposed deference to the past, try to copy techniques or forms that have become obsolete.

The sensitivity of the architect in charge of a conversion is of crucial importance, as he or she is responsible for balancing the wishes of the owners against the reality of the space. The end result is therefore the fruit of his or her ability to come up with bold strategies while also staying within the budget. This book offers a carefully chosen selection of works by architects from all over the world, encompassing refurbishments of old factories, workshops, stables, farms, mills, and other structures that have been converted into private homes.

Entreprendre la restauration d'un bâtiment s'avère parfois plus complexe qu'en construire un nouveau. En effet, il convient de tenir compte de deux obligations : celle de conserver les éléments ayant une valeur historique, et celle de prendre en considération l'état de la construction existante. Or, il est rare de le connaître avant de démarrer un projet. Par conséquent, la démarche de restauration d'un bâtiment place l'architecte devant un véritable défi, dans le sens où il est conduit à adopter des stratégies très différentes de celles employées face à un terrain nu.

Les raisons qui mènent à remodeler un bâtiment plutôt que de le reconstruire sont des plus diverses. La plus fréquente est liée à la réglementation des monuments historiques, interdisant de démolir l'édifice. A celle-ci se greffe aussi le gain de coût obtenu en utilisant la structure existante, ou encore le désir des propriétaires de vivre dans un lieu mariant le charme du passé aux commodités modernes. Dans un cas comme dans l'autre, le projet doit, à la fois, respecter ces contraintes et satisfaire les exigences des futurs occupants en fonction de leur mode de vie.

La tendance européenne, qui était depuis la fin de la Seconde Guerre Mondiale de respecter les constructions historiques, a conduit, ces dernières années, à une approche quelque peu artificieuse. En effet, dans de nombreux projets, le concept de restauration a été mal interprété : certains, qualifiés, à tort, de restauration, ne conservaient que la façade, recelant derrière un édifice entièrement nouveau. Ces interventions, ont façonné une nouvelle vision des faits : la restauration devient l'adaptation d'un bâtiment ancien aux nécessités actuelles, reléguant le dialogue avec le passé au second plan. Cela dit, si cette démarche semble assez radicale, une intervention claire et nette, employant des matériaux modernes, est souvent plus honorable que d'autres, qui, sous des apparences respectant le passé, ne font que copier des techniques ou des formes tombées en désuétude.

Dans une restauration, la sensibilité de l'architecte est essentielle dans l'art de conjuguer les désirs des propriétaires à la réalité de l'espace. De même, le résultat final dépend de sa capacité à définir des stratégies audacieuses, dans le cadre du budget fixé par le devis. Cet ouvrage offre une sélection hors paire d'oeuvres d'architectes du monde entier, un éventail d'anciens espaces restaurés, à l'instar d'ateliers, usines, étables, granges, moulins, etc., reconvertis en habitations privées.

Manchmal ist es schwieriger ein Gebäude zu renovieren als ein Neues zu errichten, nicht nur deshalb, weil Teile des Gebäudes von historischem Wert sein könnten, sondern auch aufgrund der Bausubstanz. Dennoch stellt die Restaurierung eines Gebäudes eine Herausforderung an jeden Architekten dar, da Strategien angewendet werden müssen, die sich stark von denen unterscheiden, die man bei einem unbebauten Grundstück anwenden würde.

Es gibt verschiedene Gründe, aus denen man ein Gebäude umbaut anstatt ein Neues zu errichten. Oftmals handelt es sich um Gebäude, die unter Denkmalschutz stehen und nicht abgerissen werden dürfen. Manchmal kann es auch billiger sein, eine bereits existierende Struktur zu nutzen, oder aber die Eigentümer wünschen, an einem Ort zu leben, der den Zauber der Vergangenheit bewahrt, jedoch den Komfort der Gegenwart bietet. In all diesen Fällen muss man diese Voraussetzungen bei der Planung berücksichtigen und gleichzeitig den Erwartungen der zukünftigen Bewohner gerecht werden.

In Europa war es nach Ende des Zweiten Weltkrieges üblich, alte Gebäude zu respektieren, was in den letzten Jahren zu einer gewissen Gekünsteltheit führte. So wurden bei vielen Umbauprojekten Eingriffe als Restaurierung bezeichnet, bei denen jedoch nur die Fassade erhalten blieb und die in Wirklichkeit Neubauten waren. Angesichts dieser Eingriffe an alten Gebäuden kam eine neue, aufgeklärtere Sichtweise auf, bei der die Umgestaltung als Anpassung des Gebäudes an die Anforderungen des modernen Lebens begriffen wird, wobei der Dialog mit der Vergangenheit in den Hintergrund tritt. Obwohl diese Herangehensweise sehr radikal wirkt, ist oft ein klarer und entschiedener Umgang mit modernen Materialien respektvoller als andere Eingriffe, die anscheinend die Vergangenheit respektieren, aber in Wirklichkeit nur Techniken und Formen kopieren, die längst aus der Mode gekommen sind.

Die Feinfühligkeit des Architekten, der die Umgestaltung plant, ist grundlegend, denn er muss dazu in der Lage sein, die Wünsche der Eigentümer mit dem zur Verfügung stehenden Raum in Einklang zu bringen. Entscheidend ist auch, gewagte Strategien zu definieren, die gleichzeitig das vorhandene Budget nicht überschreiten. In diesem Buch wird eine interessante Auswahl an Projekten von Architekten aus aller Welt gezeigt, unter anderem Umgestaltungen alter Werkshallen, Werkstätten, Ställe, Bauernhöfe, Mühlen usw., aus denen private Wohnräume geworden sind.

Loft in Madrid
Loft à Madrid
Loft in Madrid

The aim of this refurbishment was to transform an old sculpture workshop into a modern apartment. The transformation has resulted in a spacious loft, which even accommodates an indoor pool in the basement. Some elements from the original building have been preserved, and the exterior has been completely hidden behind white-coated metal, which also conceals the interior, heightens intimacy, and highlights the patio. The pipes have been left in view, adding to the industrial esthetic evident in the brick walls and metal beams. The height of this former workshop permitted construction of a mezzanine to house the study and bedroom. The use of U-glass translucent panels in the roof, on the mezzanine, and in some areas of the floor facilitates the flow of natural light throughout the apartment from the mezzanine to the basement.

Cette réhabilitation vise à transformer un ancien atelier de sculpture en un appartement moderne. Il en résulte un loft spacieux, abritant même une piscine intérieure au sous-sol. Certains des éléments originaux du bâtiment ont été conservés. L'extérieur est entièrement masqué par une coque de métal blanc, occultant aussi l'intérieur, pour exalter l'intimité et mettre en valeur le patio. Les tuyaux, apparents, accentuent l'esthétique industrielle, à l'instar des murs de briques et des poutres en métal. La hauteur de cet ancien atelier a permis de créer une mezzanine pour accueillir le studio et la chambre à coucher. L'emploi de panneaux translucides en vitrolit (U-Glass) au plafond, sur la mezzanine, et dans certaines zones du sol, laisse la lumière naturelle inonder tout l'appartement, de la mezzanine au sous-sol.

Bei diesem Umbau hatten sich die Planer zum Ziel gesetzt, ein ehemaliges Bildhaueratelier zu einer modernen Wohnung umzugestalten. So entstand ein geräumiger Loft mit einem Swimmingpool im Kellergeschoss. Einige der Originalteile des Gebäudes blieben erhalten. Die Fassade wurde vollständig mit einem weiß beschichteten Metall verkleidet, das die Räume verbirgt, für mehr Privatsphäre sorgt und gleichzeitig den Hof verschönert. Die Rohrleitungen wurden sichtbar verlegt, was die industrielle Ästhetik unterstreicht, die durch die Ziegelsteinwände und Metallträger entsteht. Da die ehemalige Werkstatt recht hoch war, konnte man ein Zwischengeschoss einziehen, in dem sich das Arbeits- und das Schlafzimmer befinden. Durch die Verwendung von lichtdurchlässigen Paneelen aus U-Glas im Zwischengeschoss und in einigen Bereichen des Fußbodens strömt Tageslicht durch die ganze Wohnung.

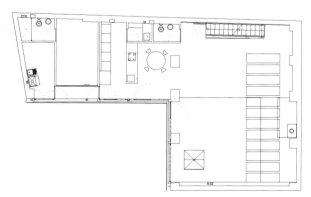

› **Mezzanine** Mezzanine Zwischengeschoss

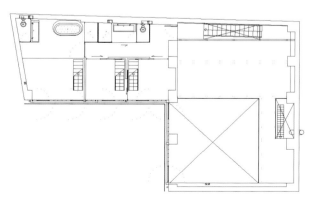

› **Ground floor** Rez-de-chaussée Erdgeschoss

The industrial esthetic of the original structure contrasts effectively with the warm decor, which includes parquet flooring and contemporary furniture.

L'esthétique industrielle de la structure d'origine contraste bien avec la chaleur de l'aménagement que dégagent parquets et meubles contemporains.

Die industrielle Ästhetik der Originalstruktur bildet einen Gegensatz zu der warmen Einrichtung mit ihren Parkettböden und den modernen Möbeln.

Residence in Belgium
Résidence en Belgique
Residenz in Belgien

The simplicity and austerity of bare cement, glass, and metal combine in this interior, which preserves the essence of its original structure and harmonizes with its surroundings. The concrete pedestal is split into two series of square platforms supported by pillars and interconnected by a metal staircase leading to the top of the tower. The renovation project involved dividing the rectangular ground floor — on a wider base than the upper storeys — into two levels to accommodate the most frequently used areas of the house: the kitchen, living room and master bedroom. The first floor contains an office, a guest room, a small garden and a meeting room. The height and position of the tower and the materials used on the exterior —Reglit double-glazed windows — turn every nook into a special place, bathed in sunlight and expose to the natural scenery.

La simplicité et l'austérité de la nudité du ciment, du verre et du métal s'installent dans cette demeure pour préserver l'essence de la structure d'origine et l'intégrer dans l'environnement. La base en béton se divise en deux séries de plate-formes carrées soutenues par des colonnes verticales, reliées par un escalier en métal qui s'étend sur toute la hauteur de la tour. La rénovation a divisé le rez-de-chaussée –rectangulaire et plus vaste que les étages supérieurs- en deux niveaux destinés aux zones les plus fréquentées de la maison: la cuisine, le salon et la chambre à coucher principale. L'étage supérieur comprend un bureau, une chambre d'amis, un petit jardin et une salle de réunions. L'emplacement et la hauteur de la tour, ainsi que les matériaux utilisés à l'extérieur – verre Reglit et fenêtres à double vitrage – transforment chaque recoin en un endroit spécial, baigné par la lumière du jour et ouvert sur la nature.

Die Einfachheit und nackte Schmucklosigkeit des verwendeten Zements, Glases und Metalls wirkt sich auf die Wohnumgebung aus, die die Essenz der Originalstruktur wahrt und in die Umgebung integriert. Der Zementboden unterteilt sich in zwei Serien quadratischer Plattformen, die von vertikalen Säulen gehalten und durch eine Metalltreppe verbunden werden, die das Haus in seiner ganzen Länge verbindet. Bei der Renovierung wurde das rechteckige und breitere Erdgeschoss in zwei Ebenen unterteilt, auf denen die meistgenutzten Räume des Hauses liegen: die Küche, das Wohnzimmer und das Schlafzimmer. Im Obergeschoss befinden sich das Büro, das Gästezimmer, ein kleiner Garten und ein Gesellschaftsraum. Die Lage und Höhe des Gebäudes und die an der Fassade verwendeten Materialien, unter anderem Reglit-Glas und Doppelglasfenster, machen aus jedem Winkel einen ganz besonderen, in Licht gebadeten und zur Natur hin offenen Ort.

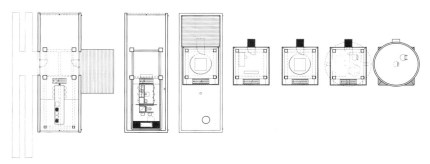

› Plan Plan Grundriss

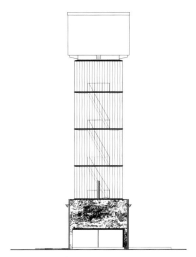

› Elevation Élévation Aufriss

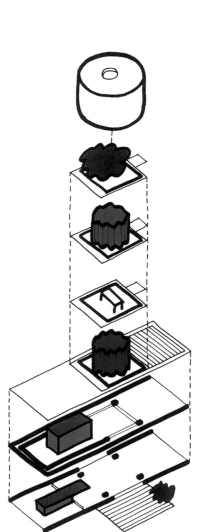

› Axonometry Axonométrie Axonometrische Ansicht

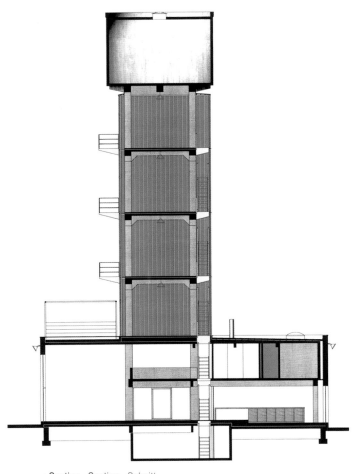

› Section Section Schnitt

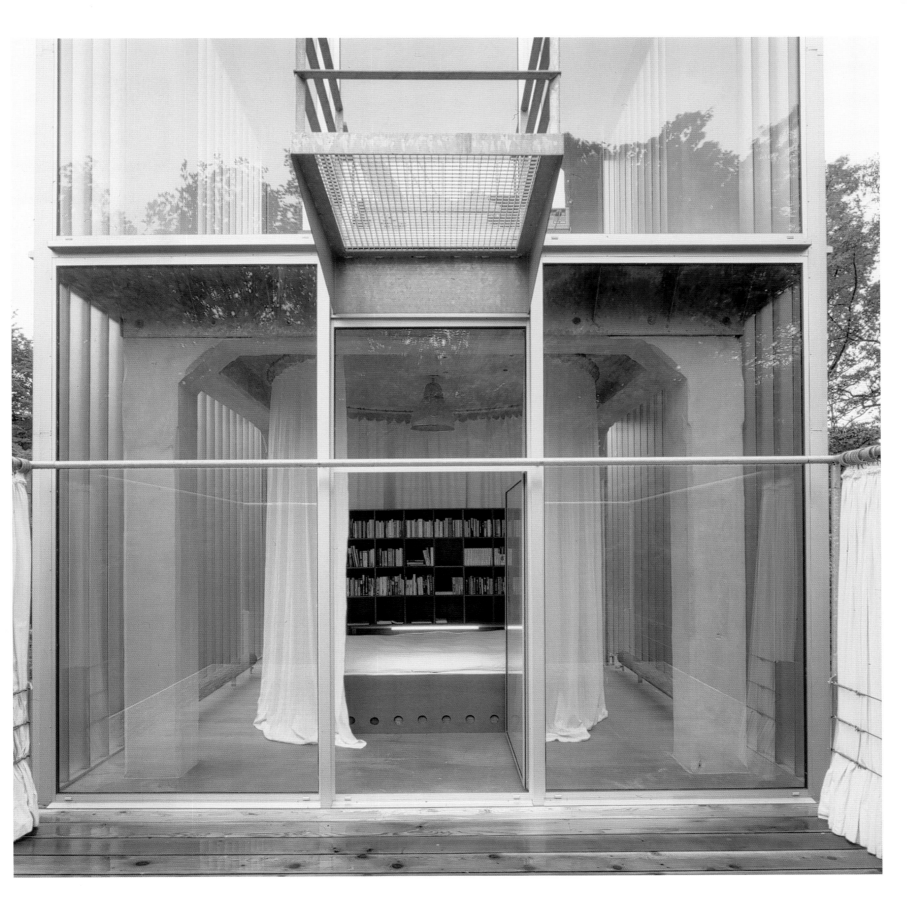

Sunlight pours through two large windows at each end of the rectangular ground floor.

Le rez-de-chaussée, de forme rectangulaire, est doté, aux deux extrémités, de deux baies vitrées qui laissent entrer la lumière naturelle.

Das rechteckige Erdgeschoss hat an beiden Enden große Fenster, die viel Tageslicht in die Räume lassen.

Blue, present on the painted walls and the tiles, is the dominant color in the bathroom.

Le bleu, couleur dominante dans la salle de bains, se retrouve sur les murs peints et sur les céramiques.

Im Bad sind sowohl der Wandanstrich als auch die Kacheln in Blautönen gehalten.

Apartments in a Bunker
Appartements dans un bunker
Wohnungen in einem Bunker

This high, octagonal bunker on Claude-Lorrain Strasse was built in 1941 and used as a shelter during World War II. In 2003 the Binnberg & Eberle team were commisioned to refurbish it into a residential block, which gained space by incorporating two new stories on top. This team of architects was fully aware that the project required a highly sensitive approach on account of the shelter's historical past. Six homes were built in all, one on each story. The great height of the bay windows allows sunlight to flood the interiors, where non of the elements recalls the former bunker's oppressive wartime atmosphere. Thanks to its fully-glazed steel structure, magnificent sweeping views over Munich, the river Isar and the Bavarian Alps can be enjoyed from the topmost duplex apartment.

Le haut bunker de la rue Claude-Lorrain, édifié en 1941, selon un plan octogonal, était utilisé comme refuge durant la Seconde Guerre Mondiale. En 2003, l'équipe Binnberg & Eberle est chargée de sa remodélation qui le transforme en un immeuble d'habitations et le fait gagner de l'espace en rajoutant deux étages supérieurs. Les architectes, parfaitement conscients de la grande sensibilité du projet et de son approche, vu le poids de l'histoire lié à cet édifice, ont construit en tout six habitations, une par étage. Grâce à l'extrême hauteur des baies vitrées, ces vastes logements sont inondés de lumière, aucun élément ne rappelant l'atmosphère oppressante de l'ancien bunker. Les deux étages supérieurs, réunis pour ne créer qu'un seul logement, offrent – grâce à la structure d'acier et de verre recouvrant tout le pourtour – des vues sur Munich, la rivière Isar et le paysage des Alpes bavaroises.

Der erhöhte Bunker der Straße Claude-Lorrain wurde 1941 auf einem achteckigen Grundriss gebaut. Er diente während des 2. Weltkrieges als Zufluchtsort. Im Jahr 2003 wurde das Team von Binnberg & Eberle mit dem Umbau beauftragt, durch den ein Wohngebäude entstand, das durch den Anbau von zwei Obergeschossen noch an Fläche gewann. Die Architekten waren sich bewusst, dass sie an dieses Bauvorhaben aufgrund des historischen Wertes des Gebäudes mit besonderer Vorsicht herangehen mussten. Insgesamt entstanden sechs Wohnungen, jeweils eine pro Stockwerk. Dank der hohen Fenster kann reichlich Licht in die Wohnungen gelangen und so gibt es keine Elemente mehr, die an die bedrückende Stimmung des ehemaligen Bunkers erinnern. In den beiden oberen Stockwerken schuf man eine einzige Wohnung, von der aus man durch die verglaste Struktur aus Stahl und Glas einen wundervollen Blick auf München, die Isar und die Bayerischen Alpen hat.

No element is allowed to recall the oppressive atmosphere of the former bunker.

Aucun élément ne rappelle l'atmosphère oppressante de l'ancien bunker.

Kein Element erinnert mehr an die bedrückende Atmosphäre des ehemaligen Bunkers.

The large dimensions of the windows allow light to flood into every corner in the interior.

Grâce aux grandes dimensions des fenêtres, la lumière inonde tous les coins de l'espace intérieur.

Durch die großen Fenster fällt reichlich Tageslicht in alle Winkel der Räume.

Annex to Gasometers in Vienna

Annexe de gazomètres à Vienne

Erweiterung Gasometer Wien

The four Vienna gasometers originally housed the city gasworks tanks. Once this sector of the central gasworks closed down, the partitions within the tanks were removed leaving only the outer brickwork shells. Architecture studio Coop Himmelb(l)au, together with three other teams of architects, presented this project to develop new forms of housing, involving the addition of three new bodies to the new structure of one of gasometers: a cylindrical core in the interior, a feature clearly visible from the exterior known as the 'shield' and a multipurpose hall on the ground floor. Both cylinder and the shield contain living spaces and offices. Sunlight reaches the interior of the cylinder from a central atrium while the shield's wide, glass facade to the north also allows light to pour in. A total of 360 homes are offered in an array of styles, from loft-spaces or 3-room maisonettes to small flats or studio apartments for students.

Les quatre gazomètres historiques de Vienne accueillaient à l'origine des réservoirs pour l'approvisionnement en gaz de la ville. Après fermeture de cette partie de la centrale de gaz, les cloisons intérieures des réservoirs furent démolies pour ne garder que les façades en brique. Le bureau d'étude Coop Himmelb(l)au, avec trois autres équipes d'architectes, conçut un projet pour développer de nouvelles formes d'habitat, en ajoutant trois nouveaux corps a un des gazomètres : un corps cylindrique intérieur, un ajout intéressant visible de l'extérieur avec forme de bouclier et une salle de conférence polyvalente située au rez-de-chausée. Les deux premiers hébergent des logements et des bureaux. Les espaces intérieurs du corps cylindrique sont éclairés par le patio intérieur ; par contre, dans le bouclier, l'éclairage vient du vitrage de la façade nord. L'ensemble des 360 habitations offre diverses formules allant des lofts et duplex de trois pièces, aux petits appartements et aux studios d'étudiants.

In den vier historischen Gasometern von Wien befanden sich ursprünglich Gastanks für die Versorgung der Stadt. Nachdem dieser Teil der Gaszentrale geschlossen wurde, riss man die Innenwände der Tanks ab, erhielt aber die Außenmauern aus Ziegelstein. Das Architekturstudio Coop Himmelb(l)au entwarf zusammen mit drei anderen Architektenteams ein Konzept zur Entwicklung neuer Wohnungen, und fügte dem bereits existierenden Gasometer B drei neue Körper hinzu: den Zylinder im Inneren, das Schild als einen auffallenden Zusatz und einen Veranstaltungssaal, der sich im Zentrum des Gasometers befindet. Im Zylinder und im Schild liegen Wohnungen und Büros. Die Innenräume des Zylinders erhalten das Tageslicht durch die inneren und äußeren Höfe und durch die historischen Mauern des Gasometers. In das Schild fällt das Licht durch eine große Glasfassade auf der Nordseite ein. Es entstanden insgesamt 360 Wohnungen verschiedener Art: Lofts, zweistöckige Wohnungen und kleine Studio- und Studentenwohnungen.

The light bathing the interior is filtered through the enormous skylight covering the communal patio area.

La lumière qui baigne l'intérieur est filtrée par l'immense lucarne qui recouvre le patio commun.

Durch das enorme Dachfenster, das den gemeinsamen Innenhof bedeckt, filtriert sich sehr viel Licht in die Räume.

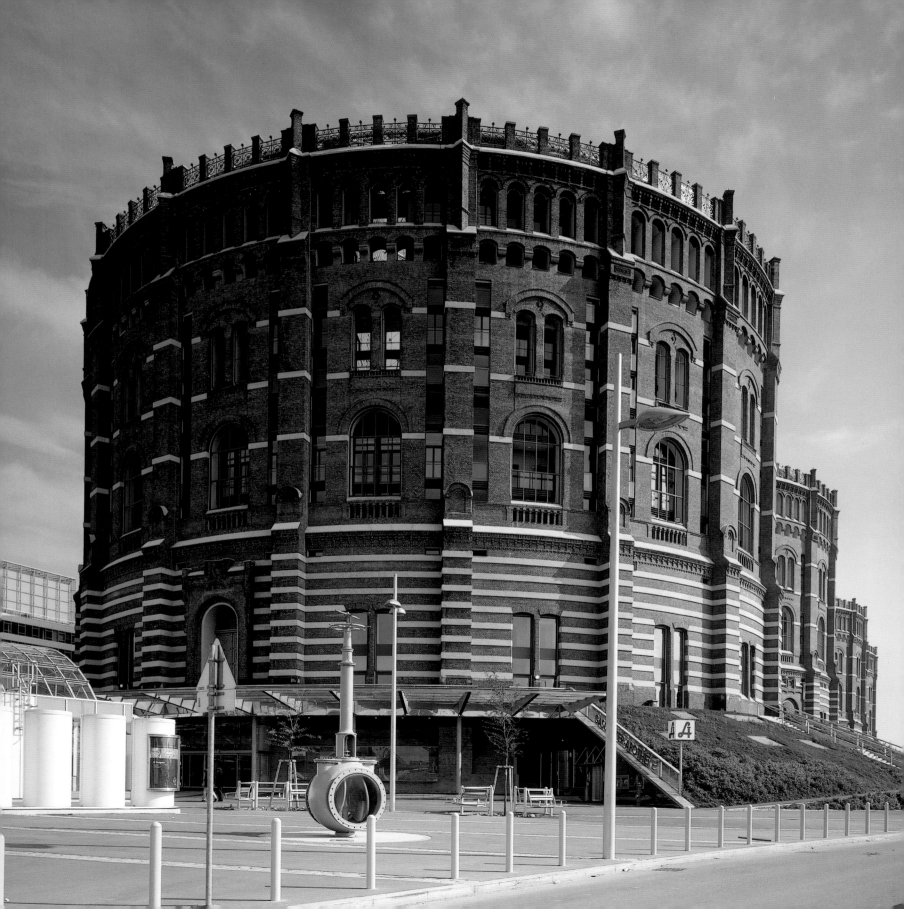

Gasometers in Vienna

Gazomètres à Vienne

Gasometer Wien

Vienna's old gasometers, built between 1896 and 1899, belonged to a time when companies considered displaying their industrial infrastructures to be in breach of good taste. Towards the mid-1980s these gas reservoirs became obsolete and it was decided they should be converted into a retail and residential complex. The architect Jean Nouvel kept the original façades intact, as a token of an age gone by, and set about designing a row of structures — initially intended to be 18, though only 9 were finally built for budgetary reasons — containing 14 storys of apartments. Every inch of interior space communicates directly with the main exterior façade: every structure has unobstructed views, either directly or indirectly, through the interconnecting spaces between the structures. Glass cladding on the sides provides an array of reflections, while allowing sunlight to penetrate inside.

Les anciens gazomètres de Vienne ont été construits entre 1896 et 1899, à une époque où les entreprises étaient réticentes à montrer ouvertement leurs infrastructures industrielles. Au milieu des années 80, alors désaffectés, ils sont convertis en un complexe commercial et résidentiel. L'architecte Jean Nouvel conserva l'enceinte intacte, témoin d'une époque, et conçut une série de 18 structures. Mais pour des raisons budgétaires, seules 9 furent construites, abritant des appartements sur 14 niveaux. L'espace intérieur est clairement défini par la façade principale : chaque structure a une vue directe sur l'extérieur par les fenêtres ou par l'espace intérieur entre les structures. Le revêtement de verre sur les côtés de l'ossature offre un éventail de reflets qui modifie les perceptions tout en baignant l'intérieur du bâtiment de lumière naturelle.

Die ehemaligen Gasometer der Stadt Wien wurden zwischen 1896 und 1899 in einer Zeit errichtet, in der die Unternehmen nur ungern ihre industrielle Struktur offen zeigten. Mitte der Achtzigerjahre wurden sie nicht mehr benutzt und man beschloss, sie zu einem Geschäfts- und Wohnkomplex umzubauen. Der Architekt Jean Nouvel ließ das Gelände als Zeugnis der Geschichte intakt und entwarf eine Reihe von Strukturen, ursprünglich 18, obwohl schließlich aus Kostengründen nur neun gebaut wurden, die Wohnungen auf 14 Ebenen enthalten. Der innere Raum ist an jeder Stelle mit der Hauptfassade verbunden. Entweder sind es direkte Zugänge oder sie führen durch den Innenraum zwischen den Strukturen entlang. Durch die Glasverkleidung der Seitenwände dieser Strukturen entstehen eine Vielzahl von Reflexen, die die Wahrnehmung täuschen und gleichzeitig viel Licht ins Innere lassen.

Both volumes were covered by a large dome made of iron and glass.

Les deux volumes sont couverts d'une grande coupole d'acier et de verre.

Beide Gebäudeteile wurden mit einer großen Kuppel aus Eisen und Glas überdacht.

Rooms receive sunlight via openings in the brick walls as well, as through the glass outer walls facing the patio area.

Les habitations reçoivent la lumière solaire à la fois grâce aux percées dans le mur de brique et à la chrysalide de verre enveloppant les façades qui donnent sur le patio.

Das Sonnenlicht fällt durch Öffnungen in der Ziegelsteinmauer und durch die Glashaut, die die Fassade zum Hof hin verkleidet, ins Innere.

The interior façade of the building penetrates each apartment, delincated by the window openings.

La façade intérieure de l'édifice pénètre chaque appartement, structuré par le cadre des fenêtres.

Die innere Fassade des Gebäudes dringt in jede Wohnung ein, umrahmt von den Fenstern.

Refurbishment of a Silversmith's Workshop

Réhabilitation d'une orfèvrerie

Umbau einer Silberschmiede

This site, virtually derelict when the architect found it, had comprised a four-story shop and apartment, and a two-story silversmith's workshop at the rear. These were separated by a small yard. The whole site occupied 4,838 square feet. Encircled by neighboring buildings, the deep and narrow site at the rear had limited exterior views out and little natural light. The clients' basic brief was to create a contemporary home suited to both work and family life that would reflect the urban fabric of the site. The clients decided to split the site into two units, one of which could be sold to contribute to the overall development cost. A natural split between the two residences was achieved by separating the two upper levels of the main building.

Ce site, en ruines à l'époque où l'architecte l'a trouvé, comprenait un magasin et un appartement répartis sur quatre étages avec, à l'arrière, un atelier d'orfèvre de deux étages. Ces deux bâtiments étaient séparés par une petite cour. Le site entier faisait 450 m². Cerné de bâtiments, l'édifice arrière, étroit et long, disposait de peu de lumière naturelle et de vues limitées. L'idée de base des clients était de créer une maison contemporaine, alliant à la fois, travail et vie de famille et reflétant la trame urbaine du site. Les clients ont donc décidé de le diviser en deux unités. L'une d'elle, destinée à la vente, permit de couvrir les frais de la totalité du projet. Deux résidences sont nées de la séparation des deux derniers étages de l'édifice principal.

Auf diesem Grundstück, das der Architekt in einem verlassenen und verwahrlosten Zustand vorfand, befanden sich einst eine vierstöckige Fabrik, eine Wohnung und auf der Rückseite eine zweistöckige Silberschmiede. Die Gebäude waren durch einen kleinen Hof getrennt. Das ganze Grundstück ist 450 m² groß. Der tiefgelegene, enge Grundstücksteil hinten ist von Gebäuden umgeben, so dass man kaum Ausblick hat und wenig Tageslicht einfällt. Die Kunden wünschten sich vor allem ein modernes Zuhause, in dem man sowohl arbeiten als auch als Familie komfortabel wohnen kann, und in dem der städtische Charakter der Umgebung wahrnehmbar bleibt. Die Kunden entschieden sich dafür, das Grundstück in zwei Teile zu unterteilen, wobei ein Teil verkauft wurde, um die gesamten Baukosten tragen zu können. So erreichte man eine natürliche Unterteilung zwischen den beiden Wohnhäusern des Hauptgebäudes.

The design focussed on exposing the shell of each of the original buildings to create a new home with spaces flowing into each other.

Le concept de design vise à mettre à nu la structure de chacun des bâtiments d'origine et d'y créer un nouveau lieu de vie doté d'espaces fluides communiquant l'un avec l'autre.

Die gestalterische Lösung war, die Außenmauern der Originalgebäude sichtbar zu lassen und darin einen Raum zu schaffen, in dem die Zimmer fließend ineinander übergehen.

The clients' basic brief was to create a contemporary home that would reflect the urban fabric of the site.

L'idée de base des clients était de créer une maison reflétant la trame urbaine du site.

Die Kunden legten besonderen Wert darauf, ein modernes Zuhause zu schaffen, das den städtischen Charakter des Grundstücks und der Umgebung widerspiegelt.

Residence in Surry Hills
Résidence à Surry Hills
Residenz in Surry Hills

The old building is one of the legendary structures in Surry Hills. Practically reduced to ashes by a fire and subsequently used as a workshop by a group of artists, an intricate restoration has brought back to life the charms of one of the city's oldest buildings. The site has been converted into an open and flexible space, a versatile loft that can serve equally well as commercial premises, an office or a home. During the restoration process the original stonework was brought back into view and this now adds warmth to the interior. The bathroom and kitchen of contemporary design contrast with the stained parquet upstairs and the beams on the ceiling.

Cet ancien édifice est une des constructions les plus légendaires de Surry Hills. Pratiquement réduit en cendres à la suite d'un incendie, puis devenu atelier pour un groupe d'artistes, une restauration complexe a permis à ce bâtiment de retrouver le charme initial d'un des plus anciens édifices de la ville. Ce lieu s'est transformé en un espace ouvert et flexible, en un loft au design polyvalent qui peut servir tour à tour d'espace commercial, de bureau et de demeure privée. C'est la restauration de la pierre qui frappe le plus dans le processus de rénovation : en effet, devenue apparente, la pierre apporte une touche de chaleur à l'intérieur. Le design contemporain de la salle de bains et de la cuisine contraste avec le parquet tinté de l'étage et les poutres du plafond.

Dieses alte Gebäude gehört zu den berühmtesten von Surry Hills. Es brannte fast vollständig ab und wurde danach von einer Künstlergruppe als Atelier benutzt. Durch eine vollständige Renovierung wurde der Zauber eines der ältesten Gebäude der Stadt wieder hergestellt. Es handelt sich um einen offenen und vielseitigen Raum, ein Loft mit einer sehr flexiblen Gestaltung, das sowohl kommerziell als auch als Büro oder Wohnung genutzt werden kann. Besonders gelungen ist die Restaurierung der Steine, die unverputzt blieben und das Innere sehr warm wirken lassen. Bad und Küche sind modern gestaltet, so dass sie einen Kontrast zu dem Boden aus gefärbtem Holz im Obergeschoss und den Dachbalken bilden.

The kitchen, dining room and living room share the same space beneath the sloping wooden beams.

La cuisine, la salle à manger et le salon partagent le même espace sous les poutres de bois inclinées qui soutiennent le plafond.

Die Küche, das Speisezimmer und das Wohnzimmer befinden sich in einem einzigen Raum unter den schrägen Holzbalken der Decke.

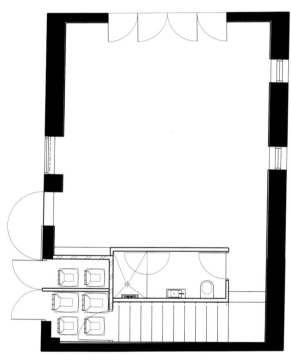

› **Lower level** Niveau inférieur Untere Ebene

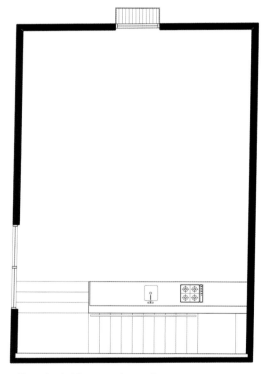

› **Upper level** Niveau supérieur Obere Ebene

Loft Vanalstine

The floor plan for this modern house, originally designed as a parking lot but reconverted into a family residence, retains certain elements from its former use, such as the brick arches separating the various spaces. A semi-transparent dividing wall allows sunlight to penetrate during the daytime, creating a pleasant atmosphere. The use of white on the kitchen walls, between a brick wall and semi-transparent acrylic panels, contrasts with the warm colours elsewhere in the house and conveys a sense of space that is heightened by the absence of doors.

Le plan de cette demeure au design moderne, destinée autrefois à être un parking, et qui héberge actuellement une famille, conserve des éléments rappelant son ancien usage, à l'instar des arcs en brique partageant les divers espaces. Un mur translucide permet de bénéficier de la lumière solaire dans la journée, forgeant une ambiance accueillante. Le blanc de la cuisine, délimitée par un mur de briques et un autre en acrylique semi transparent, contraste avec les tons chauds du reste de la demeure et imprime une sensation d'espace rehaussée par l'absence de portes.

Dieses modern gestaltete Gebäude, in dem sich einst ein Parkhaus befand, dient heute als Wohnraum für eine Familie. Einige der Elemente, die an die Vergangenheit erinnern, blieben erhalten, so zum Beispiel die Ziegelsteinbögen, die die verschiedenen Bereiche unterteilen. Eine lichtdurchlässige Wand sorgt dafür, dass den ganzen Tag viel Licht in die Räume fällt und lässt die Umgebung sehr freundlich wirken. Die weiße Küche wird von einer Ziegelsteinwand und einer halbtransparenten Wand aus Acryl begrenzt. Sie steht zu den warmen Tönen der übrigen Räume im Gegensatz und wirkt sehr weit, weil keine Türen vorhanden sind.

Brickwork arches divide the space into different areas.

Les arcs en brique divisent les différents espaces.

Die Bögen aus Ziegelstein unterteilen die verschiedenen Bereiche.

The rustic brickwork on the walls contrasts with the burnished stainless steel surfaces in the kitchen.

La rusticité des murs de brique contraste avec la surface vernie de la cuisine en acier inoxydable.

Die groben Ziegelmauern bilden einen Kontrast zu den polierten Edelstahlflächen in der Küche.

Studio in Madrid
Studio à Madrid
Studiowohnung in Madrid

This project displays all the characteristics typical of a loft. The two-story loft boasts a 3,982-square-foot upper floor that recalls its industrial past. The main objectives of the project were to maximize the exposure to natural light and distribute the space both functionally and attractively within the somewhat chaotic metal structure. The bedrooms and bathrooms were located at the sides, with the kitchen, dining room, and large living room in the center. At one end, a glass wall takes advantage of the peace and tranquility exuding the interior garden. The predominantly white walls and beams contrast with the black touches on some of the furniture (designed by the architects themselves), while splashes of red add color and vitality.

La réalisation de ce projet offre toutes les caractéristiques d'un véritable loft. Fort de ses deux étages, le loft s'étale sur un niveau supérieur de 370 m², vestige de son passé industriel. Les objectifs principaux du projet étaient de maximaliser l'exposition à la lumière naturelle et de distribuer l'espace en conjuguant l'esthétique et le fonctionnel au sein d'une structure de métal quelque peu chaotique. Les chambres à coucher et salles de bains sont disposées sur le côté, avec la cuisine, la salle à manger et un grand salon, au centre. A une des extrémités, un écran mural en verre, reflète la paix et le calme qui se dégagent du jardin intérieur. Le blanc dominant des murs et des poutres contraste avec les touches noires de certains meubles conçus par les architectes, tandis que des éclats de rouge ajoutent couleur et vitalité à l'ensemble.

Bei dieser Umgestaltung gelang es den Planern, alle typischen Aspekte eines Lofts zu unterstreichen. Das zweistöckige Loft verfügt über ein 370 m² großes Obergeschoss, das an die industrielle Vergangenheit erinnert. Die wichtigsten Ziele bei der Umgestaltung waren, so viel Tageslicht wie möglich in die Räume zu lassen und den Raum innerhalb der etwas chaotisch wirkenden Metallstruktur so praktisch und ästhetisch wie möglich aufzuteilen. Die Schlaf- und Badezimmer befinden sich an den Seiten, im Zentrum liegen die Küche, das Esszimmer und ein großes Wohnzimmer. Die Fassade, die dem ruhigen sfriedlichen und begrünten Hof zugewandt ist, wurde durch eine Glaswand ersetzt. Die Wände und Träger sind überwiegend weiß gestrichen und bilden so einen Kontrast zu den teilweise schwarzen Möbeln, die von den Architekten selbst entworfen wurden. Rote Farbakzente lassen das Gesamtbild lebendiger und farbenfreudiger wirken.

A glass wall allows natural light to flow through the apartment from the interior patio.

Un écran mural en verre laisse la lumière naturelle envahir tout l'appartement depuis le patio intérieur.

Durch eine Glaswand zum Innenhof strömt Tageslicht in die ganze Wohnung.

A large table, designed by the architects, adapts to the space. Its shape can be altered to accommodate a comfortable and elegant sofa.

Une grande table, conçue par les architectes, s'adapte à l'espace. Sa forme est modulable pour y ajouter un confortable et élégant divan.

Die Architekten entwarfen einen großen, eigens für diese Umgebung gefertigten Tisch. Seine Form kann verändert werden, um ein komfortables und elegantes Sofa aufzunehmen.

The interior garden transmits peace and tranquility throughout the house.

Le jardin intérieur diffuse paix et calme dans toutes les piéces de la maison.

Der begrünte Innenhof lässt auch die Räume ruhig und friedlich wirken.

Loft Thomas Pucher

The Thomas Pucher Studio discovered this old 1950s garage and converted it into living quarters and offices. The transformation process started by emptying the building, in order to benefit from the resulting absence of predetermined architectural conditions. The architect aimed to minimize the effects of the refurbishment by highlighting the sense of emptiness and establishing a *tabula rasa* void of design, materials or surfaces; only white paint, a minimum of furniture and an open-plan layout. This space is now the home of the architect, his wife (a fashion designer) and their son, and the workplace for ten partners, artists and designers. Living and working areas are separated by a thin glass screen and a lightweight drape, sufficiently flexible to combine spaces but also thick enough to separate them completely.

Le bureau d'études Thomas Pucher découvre cet ancien garage, au milieu des années cinquante, et le transforme en un espace de logements et de bureaux. La restauration part du vide de l'édifice et des libertés de conventions architecturales qui en résultent. L'architecte vise à minimiser les effets de la rénovation et à mettre en relief la sensation de vide préexistante, pour créer une *tabula rasa* impliquant une absence de conception, absence de matériau et absence de superficie : uniquement de la peinture blanche, quelques meubles et un design ouvert. En réalité, l'espace est la demeure de l'architecte, de son épouse (dessinatrice de mode) et de leur fils, et à la fois le lieu de travail de dix collaborateurs, artistes et designers. Les zones d'habitation et de travail sont séparées par une mince lame de verre et un léger rideau, suffisamment souples pour mêler les deux activités en une, mais aussi assez rigides pour les séparer complètement.

Das Studio Thomas Pucher entdeckte diese alte Garage, errichtet Mitte der Fünfzigerjahre, und baute sie zu einer Wohnung mit Büro um. Ausgangspunkt bei der Umgestaltung war die Leere des Gebäudes und die Freiheit, die daraus für die Architekten entstand. Die Wirkung des Umbaus sollte minimalisiert werden und dieses Gefühl von Leere erhalten bleiben, um eine *Tabula rasa* zu schaffen, die sich durch das Fehlen von Design, Material und Fläche auszeichnet und in der einzig die weiße Farbe, ein paar Möbel und die offene Gestaltung eine Rolle spielen. Heute lebt hier ein Architekt mit seiner Frau, einer Modedesignerin, und seinem Kind. Außerdem ist die Wohnung gleichzeitig Arbeitsplatz von zehn Teilhabern, Künstlern und Designern. Die Wohn- und Arbeitsbereiche sind durch eine feine Glasscheibe und eine leichte Gardine voneinander abgetrennt. So gibt es genügend Flexibilität, um beide Bereiche miteinander zu verbinden, aber auch genug Festigkeit, um sie komplett voneinander zu trennen.

Bergamot Artists' Lofts
Lofts d'artistes à Bergamot
Bergamot Künstlerlofts

This complex is named after Bergamot Station, an internationally known art center comprising a series of industrial buildings converted into forty-five art galleries, including the recently opened Santa Monica Museum of Art. Nestled between existing warehouses on a narrow site, the building takes advantage of its unique industrial setting and includes a ground-level studio and, upstairs, a gallery and three lofts where artists live and work. The fundamental challenge of the project lay in coherently respecting the industrial character of the site without compromising experimentation and innovation with forms and materials. The building, with its angular, geometrical appearance, displays mixture of materials and textures. Polished concrete floors, an exposed steel truss and metal emphasize the industrial nature of the setting, and these elements combine to create a complex interplay of space and texture.

Ce complexe tenant son nom de la Bergamot Station, centre artistique de renommée internationale, est constitué d'une série de bâtiments industriels convertis en quarante cinq galeries d'art, dont le Santa Monica Museum of Art, récemment ouvert. Niché entre des anciens entrepôts sur un site étroit, l'édifice tire parti de son emplacement industriel. Il accueille un studio au rez-de-chaussée, et à l'étage, une galerie et trois lofts d'artistes, conjuguant lieu de vie et travail. Le principal défi de ce projet est de maintenir une continuité harmonieuse avec le caractère industriel du site, sans pour autant compromettre le côté expérimental et innovant des formes et matériaux. L'édifice, aux allures angulaires et géométriques, est composé d'un mélange de matériaux et de textures. Sols en béton poli et armature en acier avec système de toiture en métal relèvent le caractère industriel de la construction, grâce à des éléments créant une complexité d'espaces et de textures.

Dieser Gebäudekomplex wurde nach der Bergamot Station benannt, ein weltberühmtes Kunstzentrum, das aus einer Reihe von Fabrikgebäuden besteht, die in Kunstgalerien umgebaut wurden. Das Gebäude liegt zwischen alten Lagerhäusern auf einem engen Grundstück. Die Planer wussten diese einzigartige industrielle Umgebung bei der Gestaltung zu nutzen, indem sie im Erdgeschoss Ateliers und Galerien schufen, und in den Obergeschossen drei Lofts zum Wohnen und Arbeiten für Künstler. Die Herausforderung bei der Planung bestand darin, eine Kontinuität und einen Zusammenhang zu der industriellen Stadtlandschaft zu schaffen, ohne dabei auf das Experimentieren mit den Materialien und auf die Innovation zu verzichten. Das Gebäude hat ein verwinkeltes geometrisches Aussehen. Die Böden aus poliertem Zement und die sichtbare Dachkonstruktion aus Stahl erinnern an den industriellen Hintergrund des Gebäudes und lassen es sowohl räumlich als auch in der Textur komplex wirken.

The materials used to clad the exterior enhance the striking nature of the angular forms.

Les matériaux employés pour le revêtement extérieur mettent en valeur l'aspect contondant de ses formes angulaires.

Die Materialien, die für die Außenverkleidung verwendet wurden, unterstreichen den überwältigenden Eindruck der winkligen Formen.

A studio and exhibition gallery occupying part of the lower floor are imbued with the industrial atmosphere of the building.

Inscrits dans le caractère industriel de l'habitation, un studio et une galerie d'expositions occupent une partie du rez-de-chaussée.

Umrahmt von der industriellen Atmosphäre dieser Wohnung befinden sich im Erdgeschoss ein Atelier und eine Galerie.

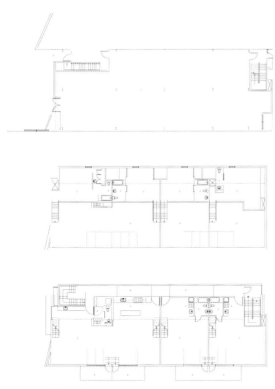

› Plans   Plans   Grundrisse

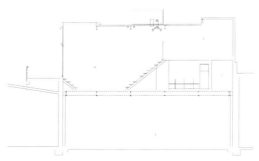

› Section   Section   Schnitt

The chimney was built from materials with a marked industrial look.

La cheminée est construite en matériaux de texture d'aspect industriel.

Der Kamin wurde aus Materialien erbaut, die einen deutlich industriellen Charakter haben.

Lofts Humboldt

The milling activity in the state of Minneapolis was the source of its capital's rise to prominence in the early 20th century, and today many of these old mill buildings have been converted into unique loft spaces. Unlike other mill district housing conversions, the Humboldt Mill condominiums offer the open spaces and raw materials of industrial conversions with a precision and lightness not normally associated with historic structures. Within the brick shell of an old mill partially destroyed by fire, nine new stories were built to house residential spaces, parking, and retail outlets. The apartments are located on the upper floors, and the top floor is divided into a penthouse, its private terrace, and a common terrace with private cabins. The new building is a thoroughly urban addition to the historic district, in a contemporary idiom that enhances the industrial qualities of the site.

L'activité meuniére de l'état de Minneapolis était à l'origine de l'essor fulgurant de la ville au début du XXe siècle. Aujourd'hui, nombre de ces anciennes structures industrielles ont été converties en lofts uniques. Contrairement à d'autres reconversions de quartiers industriels, les appartements Humboldt déclinent les espaces ouverts et les matériaux primitifs des restaurations industrielles en les associant à une précision et légèreté rarement liées aux structures historiques. Sur le coque de brique d'un ancien moulin industriel partiellement détruit par un incendie s'ajoute neuf étages abritant des espaces résidentiels, commerciaux et de parking. Les appartements occupent les étages supérieurs. Le dernier étage, réservé à une penthouse et sa terrasse privée, accueille également une terrasse commune dotée de cabanons privés. Le nouvel édifice affiche un caractère parfaitement urbain au sein du quartier historique, déclinant un langage contemporain qui rehausse les éléments industriels propre au site.

Vor ungefähr 100 Jahren hatte die Mühlenproduktion in Minneapolis eine große Bedeutung, und in der Gegenwart wurden viele dieser alten Mühlen in einzigartige Lofts umgebaut. Im Gegensatz zu anderen Umbauten, hat man in den Wohnungen der Humboldt Mill die offenen Räume und die groben Materialien der einstigen industriellen Gebäude mit einer Genauigkeit umzugestalten gewusst, wie dies bei industriellen Strukturen nicht immer der Fall ist. Innerhalb der zerbrechlichen Backsteinfassade einer einstigen Mühle, die teilweise abbrannte, dann als Garage, Lager- und Wohnraum diente, entstand ein neunstöckiges Gebäude. Die Wohnungen liegen in den oberen Stockwerken und im obersten entstanden ein Penthouse mit einer privaten Terrasse sowie eine Gemeinschaftsterrasse. Das neue Gebäude stellt eine gelungene städtische Ergänzung dar, bei der eine zeitgenössische Sprache benutzt wird, die den besonderen industriellen Charakter des Viertels unterstreicht.

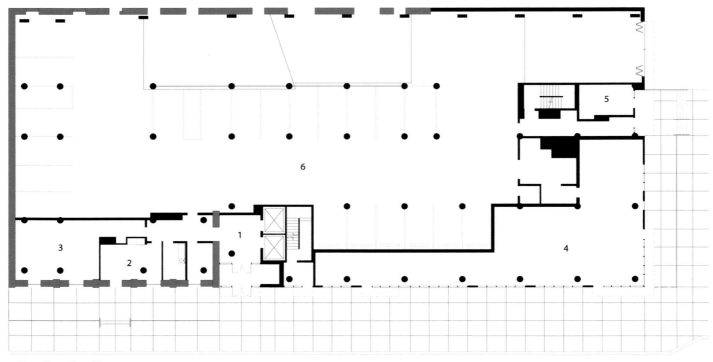

› Plan   Plan   Grundriss

› Elevation   Élévation   Aufriss

The top floor includes a terrace with panoramic views of the entire city.

Au dernier étage, la façade en retrait engendre une terrasse qui offre une vue panoramique sur toute la ville.

Die zurückgesetzte Fassade des letzten Stockwerkes lässt eine Terrasse entstehen, von der aus man einen weiten Blick über die Stadt hat.

A rich and fluid contemporary design idiom highlights the industrial qualities of this unusual location.

Un langage contemporain, riche et fluide, rehausse le caractère industriel de cet emplacement insolite.

Eine reiche und fließende zeitgenössische Sprache unterstreicht den industriellen Charakter dieses einzigartigen Standortes.

The interior blends perfectly with the outside industrial backdrop, visible through the building's enormous windows.

L'intérieur se marie parfaitement au paysage industriel extérieur, que l'on aperçoit par les immenses baies vitrées de l'habitation.

Das Innere steht in einem perfekten Einklang mit der umgebenden, industriellen Landschaft, die man durch die riesigen Fenster sehen kann.

› Elevation Élévation Aufriss

Building in Greenwich Street
Bâtiment à Greenwich Street
Gebäude Greenwich Street

Located on the lower West End of Manhattan, this former 6-story warehouse was transformed into a new 11-story residential building with an additional 4-story penthouse. The new structure is a state-of-the-art luxury property and is characterized by its 10,000-square-foot glass curtain-wall façade and open-plan loft-style layout. The integration of the existing brick building into the new steel-and-glass structure creates a visual contrast between past and present. A small seam that rises between the two buildings, articulated with a set of cantilevered balconies, juxtaposes and differentiates the old and the new, inserting an interactive space into an otherwise neutral landscape. This angular glass façade provides generous daylight and spectacular views from inside the large lofts that constitute the residential part of the tower, with their spectacular views of the Hudson River.

Situé dans le bas de l'ouest Manhattan, cet ancien entrepôt de six étages a été transformé en une nouvelle résidence de onze étages, à laquelle s'ajoute un corps sur le toit de quatre étages. La nouvelle structure est une propriété luxueuse très contemporaine. Elle est définie par une façade, à l'image d'un rideau de verre de 930 m2, et par un plan ouvert dans le style loft. L'intégration de l'édifice en brique existant à la nouvelle structure d'acier et de verre, instaure un contraste visuel entre le passé et le présent. Une petite bordure surgissant entre les deux édifices –feston de divers balcons en saillie – juxtapose l'ancien et le nouveau, tout en les différenciant. Elle insère un espace interactif dans un paysage habituellement neutre. La façade en verre, tout en angles, inonde de lumière l'intérieur de ces appartements style loft lovés dans la partie résidentielle de la tour, et leur offre des vues spectaculaires sur la rivière Hudson.

Dieses ehemalige, sechsstöckige Lagerhaus im Lower West End von Manhatten wurde in ein elfstöckiges Wohngebäude mit einem zusätzlichen, vierstöckigen Penthouse umgebaut. Die neue Struktur ist eine hochmoderne Luxuswohnung, die eine 930 m^2 große Glasfassade besitzt und wie ein offenes Loft angelegt ist. Die Integration des existierenden Backsteingebäudes in die neue Struktur aus Glas und Stahl schafft einen visuellen Gegensatz zwischen der Vergangenheit und der Gegenwart. Eine feine Verbindung zwischen den beiden Gebäuden, die durch eine Reihe freitragender Balkone gegliedert wird, stellt das Alte dem Neuen gegenüber und differenziert beides voneinander, indem ein interaktiver Raum in eine Landschaft eingefügt wird, die andernfalls neutral wäre. Diese gebogene Glasfassade lässt sehr viel Licht in die Räume fallen. Von den verschiedenen Lofts aus, die den bewohnbaren Teil des Hochhauses bilden, hat man einen wundervollen Blick auf den Hudson River.

The glass outer covering of this luxurious avant-garde property provides a wide field of vision.

La chrysalide de verre, qui enveloppe cette propriété luxueuse et avant-gardiste, permet de bénéficier d'un vaste champ visuel.

Die Glashaut, die diese luxuriösen und avantgardistischen Wohnungen umgibt, lässt den Blick nach draußen frei.

The adjacent brick building heightens the contrast between past and present.

Le contraste avec l'édifice de brique contigu met en scène la dualité passé/présent.

Der Kontrast zu dem anliegenden Ziegelsteinhaus wirkt wie eine Inszenierung der Dualität zwischen der Vergangenheit und der Gegenwart.

The polished wooden floors, steel fittings and concrete finish on the walls all combine to create a contemporary industrial atmosphere.

Les parquets vernis, les détails en acier et la finition en ciment des murs créent, une ambiance industrielle contemporaine.

Die Böden aus poliertem Holz, die Details aus Stahl und die Wände aus Beton schaffen eine zeitgenössische, industrielle Umgebung.

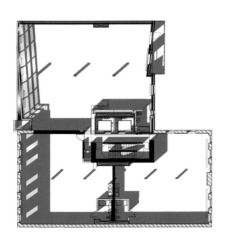

› Plan   Plan   Grundriss

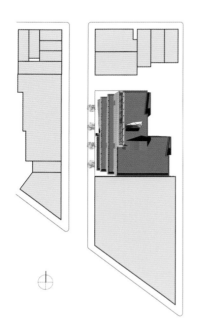

› Location plan   Plan de situation   Umgebungsplan

LA Design Center

This project, which completes the first phase of a new complex, involved the transformation of two run-down warehouses into a 20,000 square foot space, containing the LA Design Center, a furniture showroom that would provide the many manufacturers in the area with a much needed place to show their products. While it was essential to create a strong identity for the project, it was equally important not to establish an unwelcome, intrusive presence in the neighborhood. The solution was to layer the building with a richly textured, heterogeneous range of materials and screens — a new set of clothes — that seem both permanent and impermanent. By hiding, then in turn revealing and filtering aspects of the original building and the surrounding area, they emphasize the originality of the project while simultaneously enriching the public space as an outdoor foyer for the complex.

Ce projet consacré à la première phase de ce nouveau complexe, comprend la rénovation de deux entrepôts en ruines en un espace de 1.858 m² qui accueille le LA Design Centre, une salle d'exposition de meubles régionale procurant aux nombreuses manufactures installées dans cette zone, la place nécessaire pour exposer leurs nouveaux produits. Il était primordial que le projet affirme une identité réelle tout en évitant d'afficher une trop forte présence étrangère dans le voisinage. La solution trouvée consiste à construire l'édifice à base de couches issues d'une palette de matériaux et de panneaux hétérogènes et de textures riches, un nouvel habillage affichant simultanément le permanent et le provisoire. Tour à tour, ces matières en cachant, révélant et tamisant les aspects de l'édifice d'origine et des alentours, exaltent le caractère original du site tout en enrichissant en même temps l'espace évènementiel public à l'instar d'un foyer extérieur pour l'ensemble du complexe.

Ben diesem Projekt, das die erste Phase eines neuen Gebäudekomplexes bildet, wurden zwei heruntergekommene Lagerhäuser zu dem neuen, 1858 m² großen Sitz des Los Angeles Design Centers umgebaut. Dieses Design Center ist ein Showroom für Möbel, in dem viele Möbelfabrikanten aus der Region endlich mit genügend Platz ihre Produkte ausstellen können. Es war wichtig, dass das Gebäude einen starken Eigencharakter bekam, aber es sollte nicht auf unangenehme Weise unter den benachbarten Gebäuden auffallen. Deshalb verkleidete man das Gebäude mit verschiedenartig strukturierten Materialien, und kleidete es mit einer Reihe neuer Stoffe ein, die gleichzeitig beständig und unbeständig wirken. In Wechsel werden die Elemente des Originalgebäudes und der Umgebung versteckt, enthüllt oder gefiltert, so dass sie zum einen das zeigen, was sich hier einst befand, und zum anderen den öffentlichen Raum mit einer Art Foyer im Freien bereichern.

The building was layered with a richly textured, heterogeneous range of materials and screens that seem both permanent and impermanent.

L'édifice a été construit à base de couches d'une palette de matériaux et de panneaux hétérogènes et de textures riches, semblant à la fois permanents et provisoires.

Das Gebäude wurde mit einer vielseitig strukturierten Materialpalette und Schirmen verkleidet, die gleichzeitig beständig und unbeständig wirken.

It was essential for the project to produce a strong and unique identity.

Il était primordial que le projet affiche une identité forte et unique en son genre.

Es war wichtig, einen starken und einzigartigen Eigencharakter für das Gebäude zu schaffen.

› Plan Plan Grundriss

Seewürfel

This complex is composed of eight apartment and office buildings with stunning views of the lake and surrounding cityscape. The project regenerates a former industrial site into a new, attractive center for working and living, integrating its contemporary style into the historical fabric of the area. The complex is based on a concept of piazzas, created through the careful positioning of the eight buildings, each of which was designed in a different shape and size to establish a harmonious integration with the existing scale of the neighboring buildings. The structure is characterized by unique cladding materials, including gray fiber-cement panels and a specially developed silicon-bonded timber-glass-panel system. The warm, luminous interiors also comply with the highest Swiss standards of energy efficiency, by using an environmentally friendly geothermal heat pump system.

Ce complexe est composé de huit édifices conjuguant appartements et bureaux, dotés d'une vue extraordinaire sur le lac et le paysage alentour. Le projet réhabilite un ancien site industriel en un nouveau superbe lieu de travail et de vie, intégrant le style contemporain au tissu historique de la zone. L'ensemble se base sur le concept de piazzas, engendré par le positionnement étudié des huit édifices, chacun étant d'une taille et d'une forme différentes pour s'intégrer harmonieusement à la ligne d'horizon des édifices existants. La structure affiche des matériaux de revêtement uniques, constitués de panneaux en fibre de ciment gris et d'un système spécialement développé de panneaux en vitraux à joints de silicone. Les intérieurs, chaleureux et lumineux, répondant aux normes suisses les plus strictes sur l'énergie, utilisent un système de pompe à chaleur géothermale écologique.

Dieser Gebäudekomplex besteht aus acht Wohn- und Bürogebäuden von denen aus man einen überwältigenden Blick auf den See und die umgebende Stadtlandschaft hat. Ein ehemaliges Industrieviertel wurde in ein Arbeits- und Wohngebiet umgebaut, in dem der moderne Stil in den historischen, industriellen Kontext des Viertels integriert wurde. Das Konzept des Gebäudekomplexes baut auf Plätzen auf, die durch eine sorgsam ausgewählte Position der acht Gebäude entstehen. Jedes dieser Gebäude hat eine andere Form und Größe, so dass sie sich harmonisch zwischen die benachbarten Gebäude einfügen. Ebenso auffallend sind die benutzten Verkleidungsmaterialien, unter anderem Paneele aus grauem Faserbeton und ein speziell entwickeltes, mit Silikon verbundenes System aus Holz und Glas. Die warmen und luftigen Innenräume erfüllen auch die anspruchsvollsten Schweizer Normen für Energieeffizienz, indem ein umweltfreundliches, auf Erdwärme basierendes System für den Kühl- und Heizbetrieb konstruiert wurde.

The complex incorporates several different terraced areas, giving the whole site a pleasant sense of freedom.

Le complexe abrite différents patios qui convertissent l'extérieur en un environnement accueillant, respirant une certaine liberté.

In dem Gebäudekomplex befinden sich mehrere Höfe, die die Außenbereiche in eine einladende Umgebung verwandeln, die das Gefühl von Freiheit entstehen lässt.

The glass façade covering part of the building reflects the surrounding garden areas.

Le revêtement de verre, qui couvre partiellement l'édifice, reflète l'environnement paysagé qui l'entoure.

Die Glasverkleidung, die das Gebäude teilweise bedeckt, reflektiert die umgebenden Gärten.

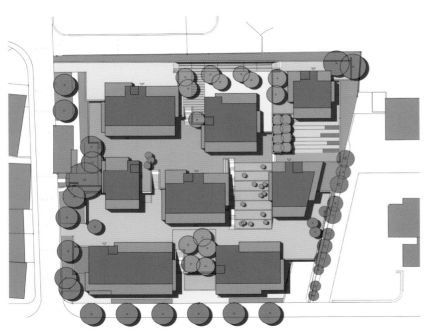

› Location plan   Plan de situation   Umgebungsplan

The carefully designed patio gardens display striking color schemes that change over the course of the year.

L'agencement végétal des patios affiche une singulière beauté chromatique changeant au fil des saisons.

Die gelungene Begrünung der Höfe zeigt eine einzigartige Schönheit der Farben, die sich im Laufe der Jahreszeiten verändern.

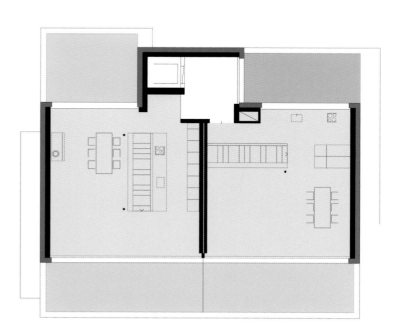

› Plans Plans Grundrisse

 Plans Plans Grundrisse

Old Municipal Mill
Ancien moulin municipal
Ehemalige städtische Mühle

The old mill in Graz, built in 1880, is exceptionally large; even its side walls are 88 feet wide. Its most outstanding features are its richly ornate residential-style facades and a five-storey wooden supporting structure. This surviving timber structure and the mill façades are now protected as listed property. High-density urban development and the lack of views made this site unsuitable for housing of a conventional nature. Lofts for a young, urban clientele were therefore considered the most suitable option, grouped on four levels enclosing an inner patio. Light permeates through the glass walls and the open façade to the north. Walkways through the timber skeleton lead to the homes. Inside, a diversity of materials, such as concrete and laminated wood co-exist with the underlying timber structure.

L'ancien moulin municipal de Graz, qui date de 1880, est un édifice exceptionnellement volumineux. Sa façade latérale mesure 27 m de longueur. Deux détails particuliers se détachent de cet ensemble : la richesse des décors de façades de style résidentiel et la structure intérieure en bois de cinq étages, qui en font un patrimoine protégé. La densité urbaine et l'absence de vues ont empêché la réalisation d'habitations conventionnelles et motivé la création d'habitats de type loft, destinés à un public citadin et jeune. Ces logements sont regroupés sur quatre étages autour d'un vaste patio intérieur. La lumière entre par le fronton vitrifié et par la façade nord, en grande partie ouverte. L'accès aux habitations se fait par des passarelles qui passent entre les poutres de bois. L'intérieur décline des matériaux comme le béton brut et le bois laminé aux côtés de l'imposante structure en bois linéaire.

Die ehemalige städtische Mühle stammt aus dem Jahr 1880 und befindet sich am rechten Mühlgraben der Stadt Graz. Es handelt sich um ein mächtiges Gebäude, das mit 27 Metern eine ungewöhnlich lange Fassade hat, die im Stil alter Residenzen reich verziert ist. Besonders auffallend ist die innere, fünfstöckige Holzstruktur. Diese Holzstruktur steht ebenso wie die Fassade unter Denkmalschutz. Aufgrund der starken Besiedlung der Umgebung und dem fehlenden Ausblick war es nicht möglich, konventionelle Wohnungen zu schaffen. Deshalb plante man Lofts für junge Stadtmenschen, die sich auf den vier Stockwerken um den großen Innenhof befinden. Das Licht fällt durch den verglasten Giebel und die zum größten Teil offene Nordfassade ein. Man betritt die Wohnungen durch Gänge, die zwischen den Holzbalken verlaufen. In den Wohnungen wurden Materialien wie Sichtbeton und gewalztes Holz verwendet, die mit der Struktur des darunter liegenden Holzes harmonieren.

The homes are reached via walkways passing through the wooden beams.

L'accès aux habitations se fait par le biais de passerelles qui courent entre les poutres de bois.

Man betritt die Wohnungen über Brücken, die zwischen den Holzbalken verlaufen.

Home Workshop
Atelier à la maison
Heim und Werkstatt

This building, dating from 1860, originally housed a grain store, but was converted into living accommodation when its former purpose became redundant. The top floor was acquired by the artist Ottmar Lerche, who converted it into his home and studio. Despite alterations to the original structure, the iron and wooden beams were preserved, as well as the texture of the vertical walls. Likewise, the mechanical external elevator, which defined the building's industrial character 100 years ago, was preserved. The owner nevertheless wished to personalize the building by filling it with a range of geometrical features of his own design. These elements are either set on a horizontal plane or stand vertically on the multicolored concrete floor. As a counterpoint to this, the dominant white background enhanced by the sunshine that pours through the skylights.

Cet édifice, construit en 1860 pour servir d'entrepôt à grains, a été transformé en habitation, à l'issue de ses fonctions industrielles. Le dernier étage a été acheté par l'artiste, Ottmar Lerche, pour le convertir en résidence et lieu de travail personnels. La restauration a gardé la structure originale avec son alliance de poutres de bois et de fer, et la texture des parements verticaux. Il en est de même pour le système mécanique d'un ascenseur extérieur, réminiscence du passé industriel du siècle dernier. Toutefois, le propriétaire a voulu personnaliser le lieu en le parant d'éléments de sa propre production : œuvres consistant essentiellement en un mélange de multiples figures géométriques baignées dans un jeu chromatique. Ces figures sont placées soit à l'horizontal, soit à la verticale sur un revêtement de ciment multicolore. En contraste, le blanc est la couleur de fond dominante que rehausse l'abondance de lumière pénétrant par les lucarnes.

In diesem Gebäude aus dem Jahr 1860 befand sich einst ein Kornspeicher, der später zu einem Wohnhaus umgebaut wurde. Das oberste Stockwerk erwarb der Künstler Ottmar Lerche, der hier seine Wohnung und sein Atelier einrichtete. Bei der Renovierung behielt er soweit wie möglich die Originalstruktur bei. So auch das mechanische System des außen befestigten Aufzugs, der noch aus der Vergangenheit stammt, und den industriellen Charakter der 100 Jahre alten Wohnung prägt. Der Eigentümer gestaltete diese Räume jedoch auch sehr persönlich, indem er sie mit Elementen seiner eigenen Produktion füllte. Seine Kunstwerke bestehen hauptsächlich aus Kombinationen vieler geometrischer Formen in einem intensiven Spiel mit den Farben. Diese Figuren sind sowohl vertikal als auch horizontal angebracht, denn auch der Boden weist eine vielfarbige Zementschicht auf. Als Kontrapunkt zu dieser Farbigkeit dominiert die Farbe Weiß, die das viele Licht, das durch die Dachfenster fällt, noch intensiviert.

Contemporary elements, such as the television or the standard lamp, contrast with the industrial look of the loft structure.

Des éléments modernes, à l'instar de la télévision ou du lampadaire, contrastent avec l'esthétique industrielle de la structure du loft.

Moderne Elemente wie der Fernseher oder die Stehlampe bilden einen Gegensatz zu der industriellen Ästhetik der Struktur dieses Lofts.

O House
Maison O
Haus O

The conversion of this old glass foundry into a family home was determined both by the layout of the new volumes as well as the site's dimensions — 2,690 square feet — its depth and other characteristics. The workshop was located at the far end of the site, reached via a terraced area. Two considerations guided the project: taking advantage of existing buildings and making the terrace a focal point, in terms of light and distribution, of the new development. A new two-story volume was built at the front, which contains the kitchen and, on the upper floor, a library. This was connected to the adjoining original buildings, containing the private living areas, by means of a one-story, glass corridor, open to the terrace, which has been converted into a garden. This tube-like space is an ample, undefined area that can be used for a range of activities.

Dans la transformation de cette ancienne verrerie en une maison individuelle, deux facteurs sont déterminants, à savoir la distribution des nouveaux volumes et les caractéristiques du terrain d'une surface de 250 m², doté d'une certaine profondeur. L'accès à l'atelier, situé à l'arrière du terrain, se faisait autrefois par le patio. Le projet s'est développé autour de deux principes : tirer parti de la construction existante et accorder au patio un rôle central, dans la distribution de l'espace et l'apport de lumière. Un volume de deux étages s'élève sur la partie frontale, abritant, au rez-de-chaussée, la cuisine et à l'étage, une bibliothèque. Le lien avec l'édifice préexistant, destiné aux zones privées, est concrétisé par un édifice d'un étage, entièrement vitré et tourné vers le patio, transformé à son tour en jardin. D'aspect tubulaire, cet espace indéfini et très ample permet de développer diverses activités.

Für die Umgestaltung dieser ehemaligen Glaserei in ein Einfamilienhaus waren sowohl die Aufteilung als auch die Eigenschaften des etwa 250 m² großen und ziemlich tiefen Grundstücks ausschlaggebend. Die Werkstatt lag auf dem hinteren Teil des Grundstücks und man erreichte sie über den Innenhof. Bei der Planung ging man von zwei Voraussetzungen aus: Der bereits existierende Bau sollte benutzt werden und der Innenhof sollte eine wichtigere Rolle erhalten. Er sollte als Verteiler und Lichtquelle dienen. So wurde im hinteren Teil ein zweistöckiges Gebäude errichtet, in dessen Untergeschoss sich die Küche und im oberen eine Bibliothek befinden. Die Verbindung mit dem bereits existierenden Gebäude, in dem die privateren Räume liegen, ist ein weiterer einstöckiger Körper. Er ist vollständig verglast und öffnet sich zu einer Terrasse, die zu einem Garten umgebaut wurde. Diese Art Rohr ist ein nicht definierter und sehr weiter Raum, in dem verschiedene Aktivitäten stattfinden können.

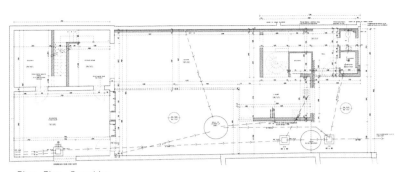

› Plan Plan Grundriss

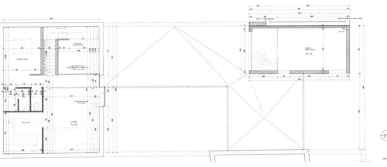

› Plan Plan Grundriss

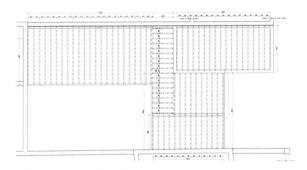

› Framework plan Plan de charpente Tragwerkplan

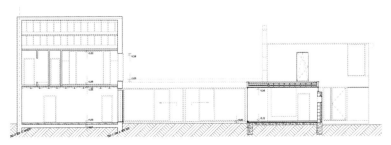

› Longitudinal section Section longitudinale Längsschnitt

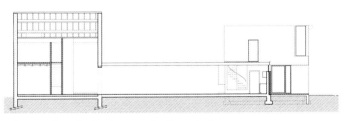

› Cross section Section transversale Querschnitt

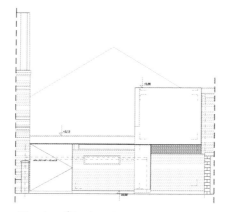

› **Elevation** Élévation Aufriss

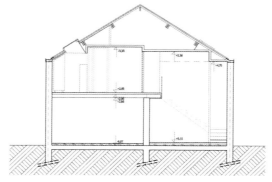

› **Sections** Sections Schnitte

The inner courtyard, now a circulation area, allows sunshine to flood into all the interiors.

Le patio, devenu zone de passage, inonde tous les interieurs de lumière.

Durch den Innenhof, der gleichzeitig als Durchgangszone dient, kann Tageslicht in alle Innenräume des Hauses strömen.

White-painted walls and pale wood floors enhance the bright, well-lit interiors.

Les murs peints en blanc et les sols de bois clair exaltent la luminosité de la maison.

Die weißen Wände und der Boden aus hellem Holz lassen das gesamte Haus heller wirken.

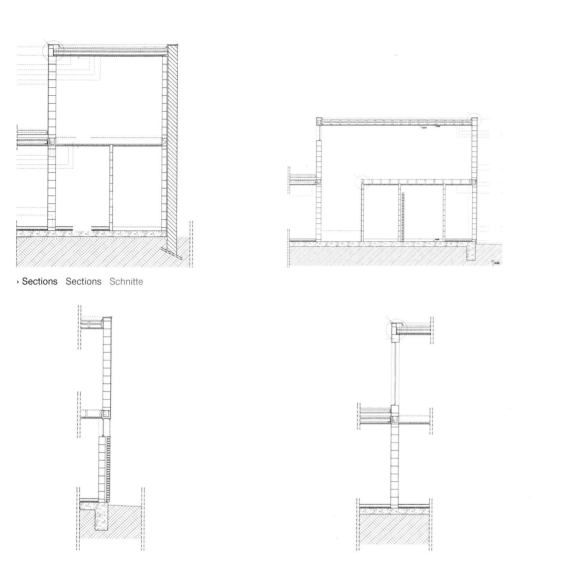

› Sections Sections Schnitte

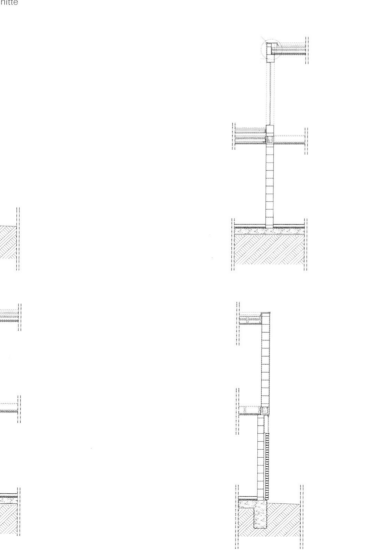
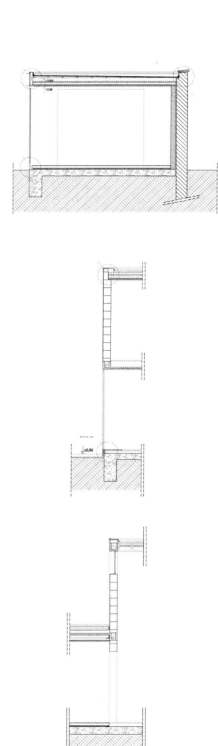

› Construction details Détails de construction Konstruktionsdetails

Former Maihak Headquarters
Ancien siége de Maihak
Ehemaliger Sitz der Firma Maihak

For many years, this complex served as the headquarters of the Maihak company, which moved to the suburbs due to the lack of space for expansion. It was decided to devote the premises to housing, but continuing to use the old production plant building would only be possible by developing a new urban restoration concept. Alterations were not masked and links with pre-existing elements were underlined, sometimes with a new interpretation. Thus, the fine-mesh metal grilles on the windows, refer to the lattices formerly manufactured at the plant, and at the same time serve as a sunscreen. The interior spaces, which were once very high, have been split up into three courtyards. As a consequence, this formerly private property has become an open, public space. Tiered layers of spacious flats and terraces have been built over the old assembly plant, and what were once offices have now become lofts.

Pendant plusieurs années ce complexe a été le siège de la société Maihak qui se déplacera vers la banlieue à cause de l'impossibilité d'agrandir ses installations sur place. Il a donc été décidé de destiner tout cet espace à un nouvel usage, le logement, mais la condition préalable pour continuer, d'une manière ou d'une autre, à utiliser l'ancien édifice de production, passait par l'étude d'un nouveau concept d'urbanisation. Sans chercher à dissimuler les modifications, des liens avec les éléments déjà existants ont été créés, en les réinterprétant parfois. Citons, par exemple, le fin treillis métallique des fenêtres, allusion à l'ancienne répartition des petits croisillons et qui sert de parasoleil. L'intérieur, extrêmement élevé à l'origine, est divisé en trois patios. Ceci a permis de transformer le terrain, autrefois privé, en espace public. L'ancien bâtiment de montage s'est vu ajouté des étages modernes échelonnés, dotés d'amples habitations et de terrasses, et ce qui avant étaient des bureaux sont á présent des lofts.

Das Gelände der Gesellschaft Maihak war viele Jahre lang der Firmensitz. Da man es nicht erweitern konnte, wurde das Unternehmen in einen Außenbezirk verlegt. Um das bestehende Gebäude für den gleichen oder einen anderen Zweck zu verwenden, musste ein neues Urbanisierungskonzept entwickelt werden. Ziel war es, die Originalsubstanz des Gebäudes zu erhalten, ohne es in allen Einzelheiten zu rekonstruieren. So spielt zum Beispiel das zarte Gitterwerk der Fenster auf die ehemalige Verteilung der Zierleisten an und dient gleichzeitig als Sonnenschutz. Das Innere, das ursprünglich stark bebaut war, wurde in drei Höfe unterteilt. So wurden aus vorher privaten Geländeteilen nun öffentlich zugängliche Zonen. Der alten Werkstatt wurden moderne, stufenförmige Stockwerke mit großzügigen Wohnungen und Terrassen hinzugefügt. Dort wo früher büros waren, befinden sich nun Lofts.

The large windows are positioned in such a way that the interior opens onto the patio whilst also retaining a sense of privacy.

La disposition particulière des grandes baies vitrées fait que l'intérieur s'ouvre sur le patio, tout en préservant une certaine intimité.

Die eigentümliche Anordnung der großen Fenster öffnet das Innere zum Hof und schützt gleichzeitig die Privatsphäre der Familie.

Some of the windows have been frosted to filter the light penetrating into the interior.

Le traitement à l'acide de certaines fenêtres permet de tamiser la lumière qui filtre vers l'intérieur.

Einige der Scheiben wurden mit Säure behandelt, um das Licht zu dämpfen, das ins Innere fällt.

The interior design was adapted to the existing structure and the spacious, well-lit rooms were retained.

Le design intérieur s'est adapté à la structure existante, tout en gardant les pièces amples et lumineuses.

Die Innengestaltung wurde an die existierende Struktur angepasst und die Räume sind weit und hell.

Rathmines Houses
Habitations Rathmines
Wohnungen Rathmines

This project involved putting up three homes on the site of an old warehouse previously used to store building materials. The new houses, built on the same space and reproducing the original construction's external appearance, are three units with dividing walls and upper levels inside a tubular shell. The architects' brief was to explore the possibilities of taking a wholly different approach to each of the three identical volumes. The ways in which their spatial, acoustic and material characteristics have been treated demostrate how subtle changes can radically transform space. In the first of these houses, built using a collection of natural materials, spatial continuity is established by the kitchen and the furniture on the ground floor, which lies parallel to the house's longitudinal axis.

Ce projet concerne la construction de trois demeures sur un terrain occupé par un ancien hangar servant à entreposer des matériaux de construction. Les nouvelles maisons, qui présentent les mêmes dimensions et caractéristiques, adoptent la forme de trois tubes enfermant dans leurs entrailles les murs intérieurs et les premiers étages. Un des objectifs poursuivi par les architectes durant le processus de design, a été de développer délibérément les zones intérieures pour exploiter le design de trois zones identiques sous différentes approches. La perception de l'espace, l'acoustique et les matériaux démontrent que les subtiles modifications de certains éléments peuvent radicalement transformer les lieux. Dans la première des trois habitations, construite au gré d'une palette de matériaux naturels, la cuisine et le mobilier, situés au premier étage – et parallèles à l'axe longitudinal de l'étage –, maintiennent la continuité spatiale de toute la maison.

Bei diesem Bauprojekt wurden auf einem Grundstück, auf dem sich ein Lagerhaus für Baumaterial befand, drei Wohnungen geschaffen. Die neuen Häuser, die die gleiche Größe und die gleichen Kennzeichen besitzen, haben die Form von drei Rohren, die in ihrem Inneren die Innenwände und die ersten Etagen enthalten. Eines der Ziele der Architekten war es, bei der Gestaltung der Innenräume zu experimentieren und drei identische Bereiche auf verschiedene Weise zu behandeln. Die Art, wie mit den räumlichen, akustischen und materiellen Merkmalen umgegangen wurde zeigt, dass durch eine leichte Veränderung einiger Elemente ein radikaler Wandel innerhalb eines Raumes stattfinden kann. Im ersten Haus, das aus verschiedenen Naturmaterialien konstruiert wurde, schaffen die Küche und die Möbel im ersten Stock, die parallel zur Längsachse des Grundrisses verlaufen, den Eindruck von Durchgängigkeit im gesamten Haus.

The ways in which the spatial, acoustic and material characteristics have been treated demonstrate how subtle changes can radically transform the space.

La perception de l'espace, l'acoustique et les matériaux démontrent que changer subtilement certains éléments, remodèle radicalement l'espace.

Die Behandlung des Raumes, der Akustik und der Materialien zeigt, dass durch eine leichte Veränderung einiger Elemente ein radikaler Wandel stattfinden kann.

› Front elevation Élévation frontale Vorderansicht

› Rear elevation Élévation arrière Hinteransicht

› Side elevation Élévation latérale Seitenansicht

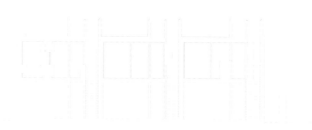

› Section Section Schnitt

› Ground floor Rez-de-chaussée Erdgeschoss

› First floor Premier étage Erstes Obergeschoss

White floors, walls and ceilings unify the room and emphasize the tubular shape.

Sols, murs et plafonds, tout de blanc revêtus, contribuent à unifier la pièce, rehaussant la forme tubulaire de l'espace.

Die weißen Böden, Wände und Decken lassen die Räume einheitlich wirken und unterstreichen die schlauchförmige Gestalt des Raumes.

Polveroni Apartment

Appartement Polveroni

Apartment Polveroni

This loft is located in an old garage that was redeveloped as private housing. Buyers were offered bare, double-story shells and allowed to decide on the layout of the rooms, flooring, and installations. The essential characteristic of this project was the permanent dialogue between the residents and the architects and designers involved in the conversion. Polveroni ended up deciding with builders exactly where the walls should end and how the stairs would fit. The boldest architectural move was to create an enormous wall that penetrates the narrow kitchen from the main living space and helps support the mezzanine studio. The walls have been covered with a layer of traditional Venetian stucco, varnished to give it a soft, warm sheen. Equally ingenious is the bathroom, at the entrance to the loft, which receives light through a glass roof, which is illuminated in its turn by a skylight.

Ce loft est situé dans un garage désaffecté et réhabilité en logements privés. Les acheteurs ayant acquis des ossatures vides sur deux étages, ont pu décider de la distribution et de la planification des chambres, des sols, des radiateurs et des installations. La caractéristique essentielle de ce projet est l'instauration d'un dialogue permanent entre les habitants, les architectes et les designers impliqués dans la reconversion de l'espace. Polveroni ont fini par décider avec les constructeurs de l'emplacement exact des murs et de l'escalier. L'intervention architecturale la plus audacieuse est la création d'un énorme mur pénétrant l'étroite cuisine de l'espace de vie principal, afin de soutenir le studio en mezzanine. Les murs sont recouverts d'une couche de stuc vénitien traditionnel, verni pour obtenir un éclat chaleureux et doux. Une autre idée de génie : la salle de bains, à l'entrée du loft, reçoit la lumière par le biais d'un plafond de verre qui à son tour est illuminé par une faîtière.

Dieser Loft befindet sich in einer ehemaligen Garage, die zu einer Privatwohnung umgebaut wurde. Die Käufer konnten die nackte, zweistöckige Struktur mitgestalten und über die Raumaufteilung, den Fußbodenbelag und die Installationen mitentscheiden. So war ein Hauptkennzeichen dieses Bauprojektes der permanente Dialog zwischen den Bewohnern, den Architekten und den Innenarchitekten, die bei diesem Umbau mitarbeiteten. Polveroni plante schließlich genau mit den Bauherren, wo sich die Wände und Treppen befinden sollten. Die gewagteste architektonische Lösung ist die riesige Wand, die die kleine Küche vom Wohnzimmer trennt und das Arbeitszimmer im darübergelegenen Zwischengeschoss stützt. Diese Wand wurde mit traditionellem venezianischem Stuck verkleidet und poliert, so dass sie warm und sanft glänzt. Ebenso einfallsreich ist das Badezimmer am Eingang, das durch ein Glasdach Licht erhält, das wiederum von einem Dachfenster aus sein Licht bezieht.

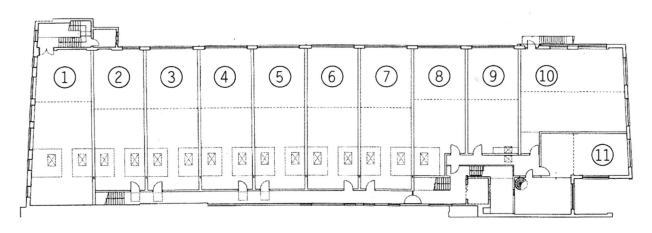

› Plan Plan Grundriss

The boldest architectural move was to create an enormous wall that dived the narrow kitchen from the main living space.

L'intervention architecturale la plus audacieuse consiste à créer un énorme mur pénétrant l'étroite cuisine de l'espace de vie principal.

Die gewagteste architektonische Lösung ist die riesige Wand, die die kleine Küche vom Wohnzimmer trennt.

The bathroom receives light through a glass roof, which is illuminated in its turn by a skylight.

La salle de bains reçoit la lumière par le biais d'un plafond de verre qui à son tour est illuminé par une faîtière.

Durch ein Glasdach fällt Licht in das Badezimmer. Dieses Glasdach wiederum erhält das Licht durch ein Dachfenster.

Loft in Barcelona

Loft à Barcelone

Loft in Barcelona

Situated at one end of an old factory, which is still used as a warehouse for construction materials, this small studio has been transformed into a loft of approximately 750 square feet. The starting point was the alteration of the floor plan — long and narrow — to convert the interior into one single space, free of any partitions. On the lower floor, which still has its original roof and is arranged on two levels, the original structure has been accentuated with wooden beams: an upper level reached via an open stairway containing a bedroom, and a lower level containing the living room, dining room and another bedroom. The latter space is multifunctional and colorful, and it receives natural light directly from the factory windows. The kitchen, situated at the rear, has an L-shaped worktop which facilitates communication with the rest of the space.

Situé à l'une des extrémités d'une vieille usine, encore utilisée comme entrepôt de matériaux de constructions, ce petit studio s'est transformé en un loft d'environ 70 m². La redéfinition du plan – allongé et étroit – est le point de départ de cette restauration convertissant l'intérieur en un espace unique, entièrement décloisonné. Le rez-de-chaussée, conservant le plafond original, avec une mise en relief de la structure première de la construction grâce à des poutres en bois, s'articule sur deux niveaux : le supérieur, abritant la chambre à coucher, auquel on accède par un escalier ouvert, et l'inférieur, qui accueille la salle de séjour, la salle à manger et une autre chambre à coucher. Ce dernier est un espace multifonctionnel très coloré qui reçoit la lumière naturelle directe par le biais des fenêtres de l'usine. La cuisine, située à l'arrière, dispose d'un plan de travail en forme de L qui permet de communiquer facilement avec le reste de l'espace.

Dieses Studio befindet sich im hinteren Teil einer alten Fabrik, die noch als Lager für Baumaterial genutzt wird. Es wurde zu einem ungefähr 70 m² großen Loft umgebaut. Der Ausgangspunkt für die Umstrukturierung des länglichen und schmalen Grundrisses war die Idee, dass ein einziger Raum ohne Aufteilungen entstehen sollte. Im Erdgeschoss blieb die Originaldecke erhalten und die primitive Baustruktur wurde noch durch Holzbalken unterstrichen. Es gibt zwei Ebenen: auf der oberen liegt das Schlafzimmer, das man über eine offene Treppe erreicht und auf der unteren das Wohnzimmer, Speisezimmer und ein weiteres Schlafzimmer. Dieser letzte Bereich ist multifunktionell, sehr bunt und es strömt viel Licht durch die großen Fabrikfenster ein. In der Küche im hinteren Teil gibt es eine L-förmige Arbeitsfläche, die eine gute Verbindung zu den übrigen Bereichen schafft.

The furniture is practical but elegant.

Le design du mobilier de la maison est à la fois pratique et élégant.

Die Möbel dieses Hauses sind praktisch und gleichzeitig elegant gestaltet.

This interior receives light through the very large window at one end of the living room.

L'intérieur reçoit la lumière par le biais d'une large baie vitrée située à une extrémité du salon.

Durch ein großes Fenster am Ende des Wohnzimmers fällt Tageslicht ins Innere.

House in Florence

Habitation à Florence

Wohnung in Florenz

By turning a former laboratory into living quarters and a studio, the interior has been remodelled into a large open space that retains the nature of the original 19th-century building as far as possible. Private and professional uses are thus carved out of a powerful industrial setting where the passage of time has left visible traces, filling gaps with modern elements that are compatible with old and new. The original distribution has undergone a number of changes, such as the removal of several walls and the addition of a bathroom, a kitchen and two balconies on the first floor next to the workroom. The lighting scheme, cement floors, brickwork pillars and copper radiators have all been designed by the architect to stress the industrial character of this space, a melting-pot of different periods lost in time.

Suite à la transformation d'un vieux laboratoire en un lieu de vie et de travail, l'intérieur a été remodelé pour devenir un espace ample et ouvert respectant le plus possible, les vestiges de la construction originale du XIXe siècle. De cette façon, les univers domestique et professionnel s'intègrent à l'ambiance industrielle qui les accueille tout en la renforçant, en laissant les traces du temps apparentes, réparant les fissures avec des éléments modernes en harmonie avec les caractéristiques du passé et du présent. L'espace initial est soumis à certains changements dont la suppression de plusieurs murs et la construction d'une salle de bains, d'une cuisine et de deux balcons au deuxième étage, à côté de l'aire de travail. L'éclairage, le sol en ciment, les piliers de brique et les radiateurs en cuivre, tous conçus par le même architecte, accentuent l'aspect industriel de l'habitation, lieu de rencontre de différentes époques éloignées dans le temps.

Bei diesem Umbau wurde ein ehemaliges Labor in einen Ort zum Wohnen und Arbeiten umgestaltet. Es entstand ein weiter und offener Raum, in dem man, so weit dies möglich war, die Überreste der Originalstruktur aus dem 19. Jh. erhielt. Auf diese Art und Weise wurden die Wohn- und Arbeitsräume nicht nur mühelos in eine industrielle Umgebung integriert, sondern man schuf auch eine Verbindung zu den Dingen, die den Lauf der Zeit zeigen, wobei die tiefsten Risse mit modernen Elementen der Gegenwart gekittet wurden. Bei diesem Umbau wurden einige Wände niedergerissen und es entstanden ein Bad, eine Küche und zwei Balkons im zweiten Stock in der Nähe des Arbeitsbereiches. Die Beleuchtung, der Zementboden, die Säulen aus Ziegelstein und die Heizkörper aus Kupfer, die vom gleichen Architekten entworfen wurden, unterstreichen die industrielle Atmosphäre in der Wohnung, in der verschiedene, weit voneinander entfernte Epochen aufeinandertreffen.

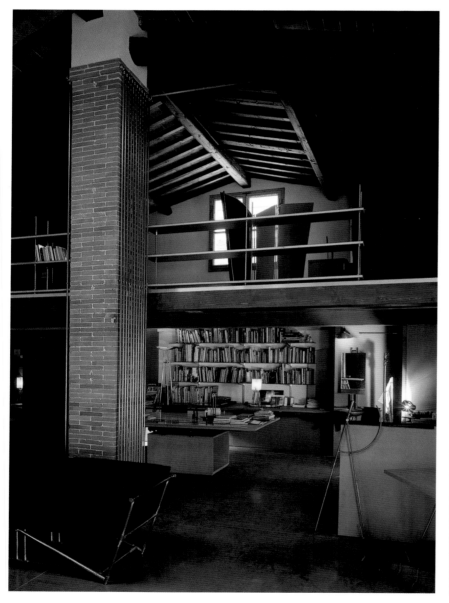

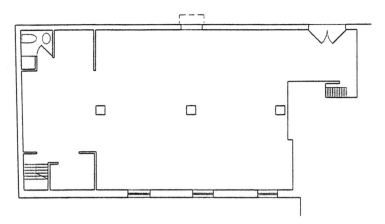

› Ground floor Rez-de-chaussée Erdgeschoss

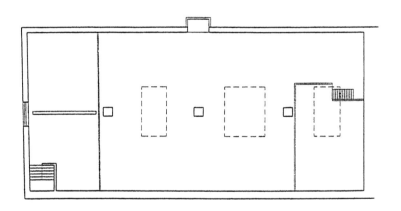

› First floor Premier étage Erstes Obergeschoss

Loft in Milan
Loft à Milan
Loft in Mailand

This original loft, situated on the outskirts of Milan in a peripheral zone where agriculture and industry coexist, is both the residence and studio of the owner and architect. The building was originally a stately home, complete with a granary, a windmill, and a series of annexed warehouses, one of which was used for this project. The structure, in keeping with the industrial architecture of the turn of the 19th-century, is characterized by the iron beams and the brick walls. The original structure has been respected in the creation of this flexible, light-filled, and perfectly habitable space. All the private areas are contained in a mezzanine — including the bedroom, the bathroom, and even a place for a future sauna —, while the studio is located on the ground floor. Natural light flows in through a large skylight and through two big glass doors, creating a warm and pleasant working atmosphere.

Ce loft original, situé dans les faubourgs de Milan, zone périphérique où agriculture et industrie cohabitent, accueille à la fois le domicile et le studio du propriétaire et architecte. Cet édifice était à l'origine une résidence majestueuse qui comprenait un entrepôt de grain, un moulin et une série d'entrepôts annexes, l'un d'entre eux faisant l'objet de ce projet. La structure affiche l'architecture industrielle du tournant du siècle, caractérisée par les poutres de fer et les murs de brique. La création de cet espace flexible, baigné de lumière et parfaitement habitable, respecte cette structure initiale. Toutes les zones privées sont comprises dans une mezzanine, y compris la chambre à coucher, la salle de bains et même l'emplacement pour un futur sauna. Le bureau d'étude, quant à lui, se trouve au rez-de-chaussée. Grâce à la lumière naturelle qui passe par un grand puits de lumière et par deux grandes portes vitrées, l'ambiance de travail est agréable et chaleureuse.

Dieses originelle Loft am Stadtrand von Mailand, wo die Landwirtschaft und die Industrie noch nebeneinander existieren, ist gleichzeitig die Wohnung und der Arbeitsplatz des Eigentümers, von Beruf Architekt. Das Gebäude war einst ein stattliches Gutshaus, zudem ein Kornspeicher, eine Windmühle und eine Reihe von anliegenden Lagerhäusern gehörten, wobei eines davon zu diesem Loft umgebaut wurde. Die für die industrielle Architektur zur Jahrhundertwende typische Struktur wird von Eisenträgern und Ziegelwänden gekennzeichnet. Bei der Gestaltung dieser wandelbaren, hellen und komfortablen Wohnumgebung respektierte man die Originalstruktur. Alle privaten Räume wie Schlafzimmer, Badezimmer und eine zukünftige Sauna, befinden sich in einem Zwischengeschoss. Der Arbeitsbereich liegt im Erdgeschoss. Durch die großen Dachfenster und zwei große Glastüren fällt viel Tageslicht in die Räume und schafft eine warme und freundliche Atmosphäre.

The building was originally a stately home, complete with a granary, a windmill, and a series of annexed warehouses.

L'édifice était à l'origine une résidence majestueuse qui comprenait un entrepôt de grain, un moulin, et une série d'entrepôts annexes.

Das Gebäude war einst ein stattliches Gutshaus, neben dem ein Kornspeicher, eine Windmühle und eine Reihe von Lagerhäusern lagen.

The glass panels in the mezzanine counteract the weight of the structure and allow light to flow in.

Les panneaux vitrés de la mezzanine contrecarrent le poids de la structure et permettent à la lumière d'inonder l'espace.

Die Glaspaneele im Zwischengeschoss schaffen ein Gegengewicht zu der massiven Struktur und lassen viel Licht in die Räume fallen.

Loft in Neukölln

Loft à Neukölln

Loft in Neukölln

This loft, spread over 2,690 square feet divided between two levels, occupies the site of a former chocolate factory. The architect decided to conserve a large proportion of the building's original features, thereby preserving its industrial characteristics. So, a magnificent brickwork structural wall, now painted white, iron girders and floor tiles can all be admired. The domestic arrangements include an open-plan kitchen and a spacious living area filled with wooden furniture on the ground floor, and the bedrooms and an enormous bathroom with an enclosed shower unit, a large bathtub and a sauna on the first floor. The two levels are connected at three different points. Works of art are set around the walls: a highly original wheeled frame, with canvases on each side, can be positioned according to the owner's choice.

Ce loft, fort d'une superficie de 250 m² répartie sur deux hauteurs, occupe une ancienne chocolaterie. L'architecte a décidé de conserver au maximum les éléments d'origine, rappels du passé industriel des lieux, à l'instar d'un magnifique mur structurel de briques, aujourd'hui peint en blanc, des poutres de fer ou des céramiques du carrelage. L'agencement intérieur prévoit au rez-de-chaussée, une cuisine ouverte et un grand salon entièrement aménagé de mobilier en bois, le premier étage abritant les chambres à coucher, une immense salle de bains avec une douche ouverte, une grande baignoire et un sauna. Le lien entre les deux niveaux se fait en trois points distincts. Les murs sont ponctués d'oeuvres d'art. Point d'orgue original : un paravent sur roulettes expose de chaque côté une toile dont le design permet d'en modifier la position au gré des désirs du propriétaire.

Dieser 250 m² große Loft auf zwei Ebenen befindet sich in einer ehemaligen Schokoladenfabrik. Der Architekt entschied sich dafür, möglichst viele der originalen Elemente zu erhalten, um an die industrielle Vergangenheit des Gebäudes zu erinnern. So blieb eine wundervolle Ziegelwand mit einer auffallenden Struktur als sichtbares Element erhalten, ebenso wie die Eisenträger und die Bodenfliesen. Im Erdgeschoss entstanden eine offene Küche und ein großes Wohnzimmer voller Holzmöbel. Die Schlafzimmer und ein riesiges Bad mit einer offenen Dusche, einer großen Badewanne und einer Sauna liegen im ersten Stock. Die beiden Ebenen sind an drei verschiedenen Punkten miteinander verbunden. Kunstwerke bedecken die Wände, und auf einem besonders originellen Rahmensystem mit Rädern wird auf jeder Seite eine Leinwand ausgestellt. Man kann seine Position nach Belieben ändern.

The light structure of the first floor and the use of glass dividing walls bestow a sensation of spaciousness.

La légèreté de la structure du premier étage associée à l'emploi du verre pour les cloisons, confère une forte sensation d'espace à l'ensemble.

Die leichte Struktur der ersten Ebene und viel Glas in den Trennwänden lassen das Gefühl von Weite entstehen.

The combination of wood and vitreous mosaic tiles alongside iron pillars makes for an unconventional bathroom area.

Le mariage du bois et de la grésite, associé à la présence de deux piliers d'acier, accentue l'originalité de cette salle de bains peut conventionnelle.

Die Kombination aus Holz, Steinzeug und den Eisenträgern gibt dem Bad eine ungewöhnliche Note.

Attic in Berlin
Attique à Berlin
Dachgeschoss in Berlin

This 2,365 square-foot attic space sits atop a listed, early 19th-century industrial building. This *hinterhouse* — a building whose main façade gives way to an inner courtyard — was refurbished between 1998 and 2000. During this restructuring, the roof of the old store-house was dismantled and replaced with a spectacular dome. Iron beams spanning the attic roof were installed to support the new structure, which weighed over two and half tons. The abundant light now entering the building has made it possible to create an indoor garden. In addition, an iron staircase leading to the terrace was installed, strengthening the connection with the exterior. The service elevator fitted to the front of the building was completely overhauled and shrouded in a glass structure.

Cet attique de 220 m² couronne un édifice industriel du début du XIXe siècle, classé monument historique. Cet *hinterhaus*, mot allemand désignant un bâtiment dont la façade arrière donne sur une cour intérieure, a été restauré entre les années 1998 et 2000. Suite à cette intervention, la toiture de l'ancien entrepôt a été démantelée et remplacée par une coupole spectaculaire dont le poids atteint plus de deux tonnes et demie. Pour la soutenir, on a installé deux poutres d'acier traversant le plafond de l'attique de part en part. La lumière abondante, qui inonde désormais la nouvelle demeure, a permis la création d'un jardin intérieur. En outre, un escalier d'acier qui mène à la terrasse, accentue le lien avec l'extérieur. Le monte-charge collé à la façade, a été entièrement restauré et enveloppé d'une structure de verre.

Dieses 220 m² große Dachgeschoss in einem Industriegebäude vom Beginn des 19. Jh. steht unter Denkmalschutz. Das Hinterhaus, dessen Fassade zum Innenhof liegt, wurde zwischen 1998 und 2000 renoviert. Bei diesem Eingriff wurde das Dach des alten Lagerhauses abgerissen und durch eine spektakuläre Kuppel ersetzt. Um die über zweieinhalb Tonnen schwere Struktur zu stützen, wurden Eisenträger montiert, die die Decke der Dachwohnung durchqueren. Da sehr viel Licht in das Dachgeschoss fällt, war es möglich, in einem Teil der Wohnung einen Wintergarten zu schaffen. Außerdem wurde eine Stahltreppe montiert, die zur Terrasse führt, so dass eine stärkere Verbindung nach außen entsteht. Der Lastenaufzug an der Fassade wurde vollständig restauriert und mit einer Glasstruktur verkleidet.

240

Loft Moneo

The old, wooden pillars and beams in this home and office, stalwart survivors of times past, are both the backbone of the structure and the distinguishing traits of its outer face, reflecting the union of the past and present. The original skeleton runs diagonally across the house's triangular floor plan and seems to outline, quite naturally, the dining room, kitchen, living room, library and office. All the private areas are distributed over the first floor: master bedroom, bathroom and children's bedroom. The living room and dining room feature two remarkable, solid wood, antique tables that match the beams setting them off to advantage against the lighter colors of the steel and metal. Parquet flooring creates continuity and warmth, although rugs are also used to mark off different settings.

Les piliers et poutres de bois de cette demeure et du bureau, qui ont survécu aux temps qui passe, constituent la colonne vertébrale de la construction et dessinent les traits de son visage extérieur, reflet de l'alliance entre le passé et le présent. L'ossature initiale s'étend en diagonale à travers le sol triangulaire de la maison, définissant presque naturellement, la salle à manger, la cuisine, la salle de séjour, la bibliothèque et le bureau. L'étage supérieur abrite les sphères privées de la maison, la chambre à coucher des propriétaires, la salle de bains et la chambre d'enfants. La salle de séjour et la salle à manger sont mises en valeur par la présence de tables anciennes en bois robuste, en harmonie avec les poutres et les piliers, s'accordant avec des tons plus clairs, comme l'acier et le métal. La présence du parquet imprègne l'espace de continuité et d'intimité, accentuées par divers tapis créant des univers différents.

Die Säulen und Holzbalken dieser kombinierten Wohn- und Arbeitsumgebung haben den Jahren widerstanden. Sie bilden das Rückgrat des Gebäudes und prägen dessen Gesichtszüge, die die Verbindung der Vergangenheit mit der Gegenwart widerspiegeln. Das Originalskelett erstreckt sich diagonal über den dreieckigen Boden des Hauses und definiert mühelos das Speisezimmer, die Küche, das Wohnzimmer, die Bibliothek und das Büro. Das Obergeschoss beherbergt die privateren Räume des Hauses, also das Schlafzimmer, das Bad und das Kinderzimmer. Das Wohnzimmer und das Esszimmer werden von zwei alten Tischen aus robustem Holz beherrscht, die gut zu den Dachbalken und den Säulen passen und die helleren Materialien wie Stahl und Metall ergänzen. Der Parkettfußboden lässt die Räume durchgehend und freundlich wirken. Verschiedene Teppiche setzen Akzente, unterteilen die Fläche und schaffen unterschiedliche Bereiche.

The rich color scheme that dominates this loft is greatly enhanced by the abundance of natural light entering from outside.

La richesse chromatique qui domine ce loft, est fortement rehaussée par l'abondante lumière naturelle issue de l'extérieur.

Die reichen Farben, die dieses Loft beherrschen, werden durch das intensive Tageslicht, das von raußen in die Räume fällt, noch betont.

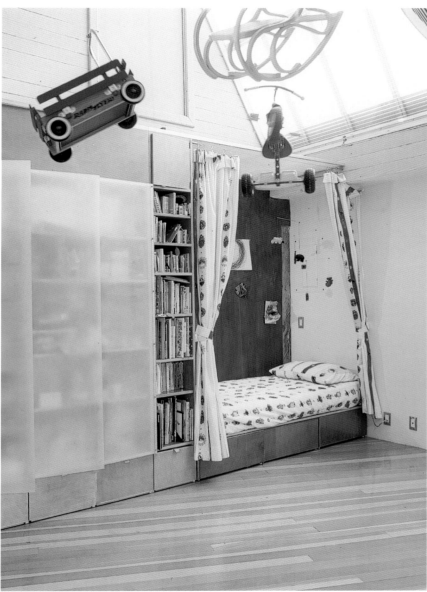

The open kitchen is compact, but fully equipped.

Malgré sa forme compacte, la cuisine ouverte répond à tous les besoins de l'occupant.

Die offene Küche ist zwar relativ kompakt gehalten, erfüllt aber dennoch alle Ansprüche des Benutzers.

Cantallops House

Maison Cantallops

Haus Cantallops

This project involved the restoration of a farm and its outbuildings in La Garrotxa Volcanic Zone Natural Park, with two clear objectives in mind: to convert the old barn into a new house and to fit out the farm itself as a rural tourism center. In both cases, the architect has complied with strict local building regulations of the natural park and taken into account the excellent views on offer. The open façade of the stables was enclosed by large windows to provide unlimited views of the surrounding countryside and forests. In this way, all the bedrooms are in direct contact with nature, and enjoy changing effects of light as the day progresses. Both buildings have been painted bright red, echoing one of the natural hues found in the local volcanic rock formations and setting off the dark colors of the original stonework.

Ce projet aborde la restauration de plusieurs fermes situées dans un parc naturel de la région volcanique de la Garrotxa. Il s'en dégage deux objectifs principaux : convertir l'ancienne étable en une nouvelle maison et adapter la ferme en fonction de la demande du tourisme rural. Dans les deux cas, l'architecte à tenu compte à la fois des règlements stricts en vigueur dans le parc naturel et des vues qu'il offre. La façade ouverte de l'étable a été fermée par une baie vitrée pour bénéficier des vues sur la campagne et les bois alentour. De ce fait, toutes les chambres de la maison sont directement en contact avec l'environnement, pouvant bénéficier des variations de lumière tout au long de la journée. Pour exalter les couleurs sombres de la pierre volcanique de la vieille étable, les deux édifices sont peints en rouge intense, couleur des pierres volcaniques de la zone.

Während dieses Bauprojektes wurden verschiedene Gehöfte im Naturpark der von Vulkanen geprägten Region La Garrotxa restauriert. Dabei verfolgte man zwei Ziele. Man wollte den ehemaligen Stall in ein neues Wohnhaus umbauen und das Gehöft so gestalten, dass es für den Tourismus auf dem Lande genutzt werden kann. Die Architekten mussten dabei die strengen Vorschriften des Naturparks einhalten, und gleichzeitig durfte der wundervolle Blick auf die Umgebung nicht verloren gehen. Deshalb schuf man an der Fassade des ehemaligen Stalls eine Glaswand, so dass man den schönen Blick auf die umliegenden Felder und Wälder genießen kann. Alle Schlafzimmer des Hauses sind direkt mit der Umgebung verbunden und alle Veränderungen des Tageslichts spiegeln sich im Tagesverlauf in diesen Räumen wider. Um die dunklen Farben des Vulkangesteins im ehemaligen Stall zu unterstreichen, wurden beide Gebäude in einem intensiven Rot gestrichen; eine Farbe, die für die vulkanischen Steine der Region typisch ist.

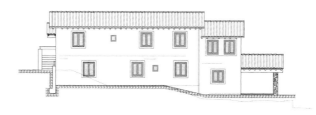

› Side elevation   Élévation latérale   Seitenansicht

› Side elevation   Élévation latérale   Seitenansicht

› Rear elevation   Élévation arrière   Hinteransicht

› Front elevation   Élévation frontale   Vorderansicht

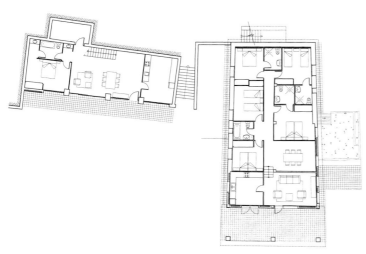

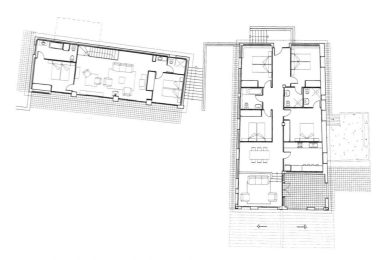

› Ground floor   Rez-de-chaussée   Erdgeschoss

› First floor   Premier étage   Erstes Obergeschoss

The front of the stables was enclosed by a new glass façade, to provide views of the surrounding countryside and preserve the building's agricultural character.

L'ancienne façade de l'étable est fermée par une paroi de verre pour continuer de voir l'extérieur et garder le caractère agricole de l'édifice.

Die Fassade des ehemaligen Stalls wurde mit einer Glaswand geschlossen, um so den Blick freizuhalten und das ländliche Aussehen des Gebäudes zu wahren.

East Hotel

Before its reconversion, the building currently housing the East Hotel — in the St. Pauli district and very close to the Reeperbahn quarter with its clubs and theatres — used to be a foundry. Since it opened in late 2004, the hotel has become a part of the vibrant day and night life in the area. A new wing was built on to the old industrial plant; the original building holds twelve rooms above the main restaurant, which opens onto a luxuriant interior garden through impressive glass doors. A spectaular sculptured wall hides the wine cellar and bar, where poufs are provided to sit on. The new volume accommodates the remaining rooms as well as the conference rooms and halls. The main building's industrial past exercised a strong influence in this project, where the designers also took inspiration from the blend of Eastern and Western cultures.

Avant sa restauration, cet édifice était une fonderie. Il abrite aujourd'hui le East Hotel, situé dans le quartier de St. Pauli à proximité de la zone des théâtres et des clubs de Reeperbahn. Depuis son inauguration à la fin de 2004, l'hôtel est devenu un des centres névralgiques de la vie nocturne et diurne de cette zone. Un volume nouveau a été ajouté à l'ancienne usine. Celle-ci accueille douze pièces, construites au-dessus du restaurant principal, ouvert grâce à d'imposantes portes de verresur un luxuriant jardin intérieur. Un spectaulaire mur-sculpture masque la cave et le bar débordant de poufs. Le nouveau volume héberge les autres chambres et les salles de réunions ou séminaires. Le passé industriel de l'édifice principal a influencé le projet des designers, qui se sont également inspirés de la fusion entre les cultures orientales et occidentales.

Dieses Gebäude, in dem sich heute das East Hotel im Viertel St. Pauli ganz in der Nähe der Theater und Bars der Reeperbahn befindet, war einst eine Gießerei. Seit seiner Eröffnung Ende 2004 ist das Hotel zu einem der wichtigsten Punkte des täglichen und nächtlichen Lebens in diesem Teil der Stadt geworden. Im alten Gebäudeteil, der ehemaligen Fabrik, schufen die Architekten zwölf Zimmer über dem Hauptrestaurant, von dem aus man durch riesige Glastüren in einen üppigen Garten schaut. An dieses alte Gebäude baute man einen neuen Komplex an. Eine auffallende Wand mit plastischen Formen verbirgt die Bodega und eine Bar voller Sitzwürfel. Im neuen Anbau liegen die übrigen Zimmer und die Konferenz- und Veranstaltungsräume. Die Planer ließen sich bei ihrer kreativen Arbeit von der industriellen Vergangenheit des Gebäudes und von einer Fusion zwischen der westlichen und östlichen Kultur inspirieren.

The East Hotel revolves around a great central space, joined to an indoor patio through four impressive double glass doors.

Le East Hotel évolue autour d'un grand espace central qui communique avec un patio intérieur grâce à quatre imposantes doubles portes de verre.

Mittelpunkt des East Hotels ist ein großer, zentraler Raum, in dem vier riesige Glastüren eine Verbindung zum Innenhof schaffen.

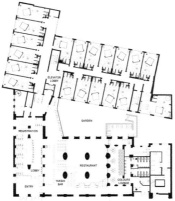

› **Lower level** Niveau inférieur Untere Ebene

› Upper level Niveau supérieur Obere Ebene

Cristofolini House
Maison Cristofolini
Cristofolini Haus

This old farmhouse, built in 1761, has been refurbished and converted into a home, while showing the greatest respect towards the traditional architecture of southern Switzerland. The architect decided to maintain the original structure, taking other farmhouses in the vicinity as a model but without losing sight of modern trends. In order to recapture the original interiors, a number of inner dividing walls — built more recently — were pulled down. The space once devoted to storing forage for cattle has been restored, and now serves as a 15 foot-high entrance hallway, while the main façade has been refurbished in the typical Vaud Canton style, complete with its traditional four-square door. The visual impact of these wooden structures — doors, stairs, rafters and handrails — is emphasized by a specially designed lighting scheme, with fixtures that pick out each feature and endow it with sculptural qualities while, at the same time, illuminating circulation areas.

Cette ancienne ferme, construite en 1761, a été restaurée et reconvertie en habitation, en respectant l'architecture traditionnelle du sud de la Suisse. L'architecte a décidé de conserver la structure d'origine en prenant modèle sur les fermes existantes dans la zone, tout en tenant compte du présent. Pour retrouver l'état original de l'intérieur, on a démoli quelques cloisons, fruits d'aménagements postérieurs à la construction. L'espace, destiné autrefois à engranger le fourrage pour le bétail, est restauré en un vestibule de 15 m de haut. La façade est rénovée dans le style des exploitations agricoles du canton de Vaud où prédomine la grande porte à quatre modules. Pour exalter l'impact visuel des structures de bois – portes, escaliers, poutres et mains courantes –, on a conçu un système d'éclairage à base de foyers lumineux qui les façonnent au point de les métamorphoser en sculptures, tout en éclairant les zones de passage.

Beim Umbau dieses ehemaligen Bauernhauses aus dem Jahr 1761 zollte man der traditionellen Architektur im Süden der Schweiz großen Respekt. Der Architekt entschied sich für die Erhaltung der Originalstruktur und ließ sich von den existierenden Bauernhäusern der Region inspirieren, war aber auch für moderne Einflüsse offen. Um den Originalzustand im Inneren des Hauses wieder herzustellen, wurden einige Trennwände abgerissen, die zu einem späteren Zeitpunkt eingezogen worden sind. Der Futterraum wurde zu einer 15 m hohen Vorhalle umgebaut und die Fassade im Stil der Bauernhäuser im Kanton Vaud restauriert. Diese Fassaden werden von einem vierteiligen, großen Tor beherrscht. Um die Holzstruktur, also die Türen, Treppen, Balken und Geländer, visuell hervorzuheben, wurde ein Beleuchtungssystem mit Scheinwerfern geschaffen, die die Durchgangsbereiche beleuchten und die Holzelemente skulpturell wirken lassen.

The white-painted walls convey a greater sense of space.

Tous les murs sont peints en blanc pour transmettre une sensation de plus grande amplitude.

Alle Wände sind weiß gestrichen, so dass der Eindruck von mehr Weite entsteht.

› Sections Sections Schnitte

› Elevation Élévation Aufriss

On the first floor, the solid panels on the façade mark the limits of the space.

Au premier étage, les solides panneaux de la façade définissent les dimensions de l'espace.

Im ersten Stock bestimmen die soliden Paneele der Fassade die Dimensionen des Raumes.

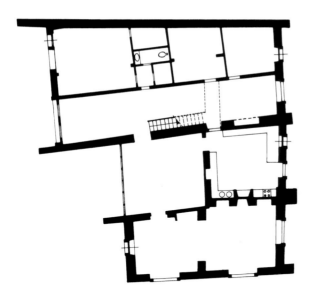

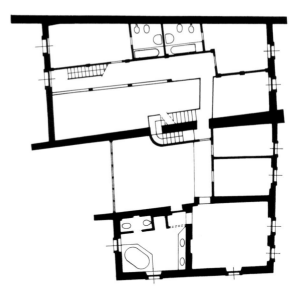

› First floor   Premier étage   Erstes Obergeschoss

› Second floor   Deuxième étage   Zweites Obergeschoss

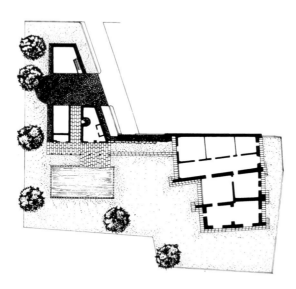

› Location plan   Plan de situation   Umgebungsplan

Suppenküche

The Suppenküche building, constructed in the 1830s as a shelter for poor people, was built in a style that had its heyday during the industrial revolution. It continued with its original function until 1920 and was then converted into small industrial workshops after the Second World War. At the turn of the 21st century, it was put to residential use. Nowadays, after a further refurbishment, the building contains seven lofts, some used as offices and others combining homes and studios. The spirit of the original building has been preserved throughout, whilst adapting the space to fulfil the requirements of modern and comfortable homes, with new fixtures, parquet floors and extra partitions to differentiate specific areas. The large fireplace, which was formerly used for cooking as well as heating, and the solid, functional brick walls have now been converted into of great historic value.

L'édifice Suppenküche, construit dans les années 1830, hébergeait un centre d'accueil pour personnes démunies, un type de construction qui connut son apogée lors de la révolution industrielle. Occupant ses fonctions premières jusqu'en 1920, il est réhabilité après la II Guerre Mondiale, et abrite, à l'époque, des petits ateliers industriels. A l'orée du XXIe siècle, il devient résidentiel. Aujourd'hui, après une ultime réhabilitation, l'édifice accueille sept lofts, hébergeant des bureaux et des formules conjuguant habitations et studios. Toutes ces restaurations ont essayé de conserver l'essence de l'édifice premier, tout en adaptant les espaces aux nécessités d'un foyer moderne et confortable, doté de nouvelles installations, de parquets et de cloisons pour différencier les zones les unes des autres. La grande cheminée, qui servait tour à tour pour cuisiner ou pour chauffer les pièces, comme les solides murs de brique, dotés autrefois d'une fonction bien définie, sont aujourd'hui des éléments de décoration d'un grand valeur historique.

In diesem Gebäude, das ungefähr 1830 erbaut wurde, befand sich einst eine der Suppenküchen aus dem Zeitalter der industriellen Revolution. Das Haus stand den armen Menschen bis zum Jahr 1920 offen. Nach dem Zweiten Weltkrieg siedelten sich kleine Werkstätten in dem Gebäude an. Anfang des 21. Jh. wurde es zu einem Wohnhaus umgebaut und bei der letzten Renovierung brachte man sieben Lofts, Büros und kleine Studiowohnungen in dem Gebäude unter. In all diesen Räumen versuchte man, die Essenz des ursprünglichen Gebäudes zu erhalten und sie gleichzeitig an die Anforderungen eines modernen und komfortablen Heims anzupassen. Sie wurden mit neuen Installationen, Parkett und einigen Raumteilern, die einzelne Bereiche voneinander abgrenzen, ausgestattet. Der große Kamin, der sowohl zum Heizen als auch zum Kochen diente, und die soliden Ziegelsteinmauern, die vorher eine konkrete Funktion erfüllten, sind nun zu einem Dekorationselement von großem historischen Wert geworden.

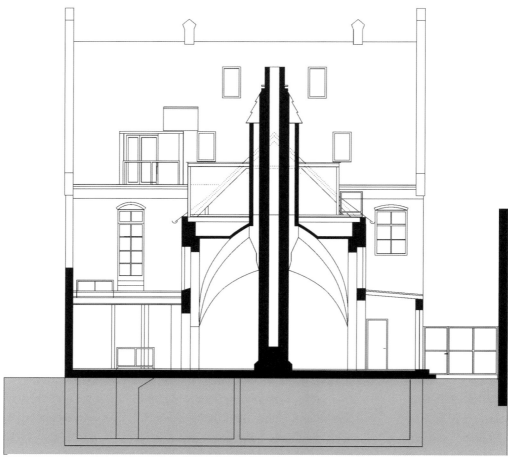

› Cross section   Section transversale   Querschnitt

Converting historical buildings into housing is a practical way of reusing premises that would otherwise become derelict.

La réhabilitation d'édifices historiques en habitations est une solution pratique permettant de tirer parti de constructions qui, sinon, resteraient à l'état d'abandon.

Der Umbau historischer Gebäude in Wohnungen stellt eine praktische Lösung dar, um alte Gebäude vor dem Verfall zu bewahren.

› Longitudinal sections   Sections longitudinales   Längsschnitte

The Suppenküche was built during the 1830s as a shelter for the poor, unemployed or homeless.

L'édifice Suppenküche, construit au cours des années 1830, était un centre d'accueil pour personnes démunies.

Das Gebäude der Suppenküche wurde um 1830 errichtet und es beherbergte zu dieser Zeit eine Armenküche.

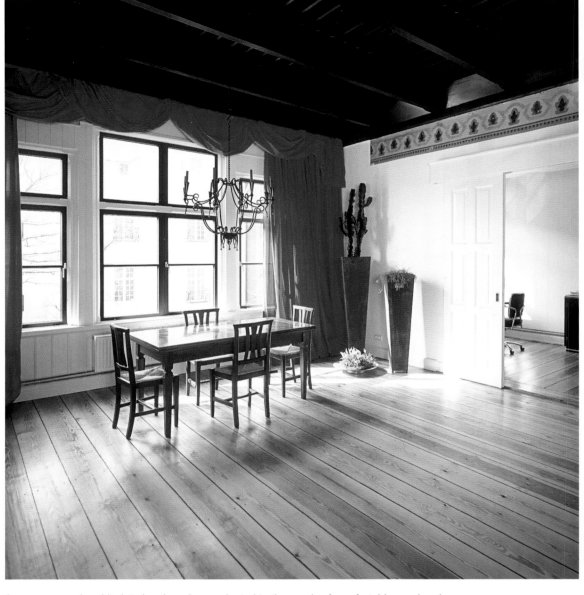

The most characteristic features of the original building have been preserved and its interiors have been adapted to the needs of comfortable, modern homes.

Les éléments caractéristiques de l'édifice d'origine sont conservés et les espaces adaptés aux besoins d'une habitation moderne et confortable.

Die charakteristischen Elemente des Originalgebäudes blieben erhalten und die Räume wurden in eine moderne und komfortable Wohnumgebung umgestaltet.

This modern kitchen, set between two levels, is highly attractive but also supremely functional.

Cette cuisine moderne, placée entre deux niveaux, ne perd en rien son esthétique et sa fonctionnalité.

Obwohl sich diese moderne Küche über zwei Ebenen erstreckt, blieb ihre Ästhetik und Funktionalität erhalten.

Padley Mill
Moulin Padley
Padley Mühle

This old mill in Padley Canyon, on top of a hill of brownish-gray and pinkish sandstone, is now a country house. The restoration took care to preserve essential elements: the rough-hewn sandstone walls which merge into the surroundings, and the original medieval slate roof. At the same time, the project sought to introduce contemporary features into the setting, using stone from the area, put in place by local craftsmen: the mill pond was restored, for decorative purposes, and the old industrial architecture was given a distinctive minimalist feel. The scene sets up a fascinating dialogue, derived from its unbroken link with its historic past.

Dans le canyon de Padley, cet ancien moulin, situé sur une colline de grès et dont les teintes se déclinent dans un camaïeu de gris brun et de rose, est devenu aujourd'hui, une maison de campagne. La restauration de ce moulin a permis de sauvegarder deux éléments essentiels : les murs en grès rugueux, permettant d'intégrer le corps de la construction à la nature environnante et le toit en ardoise, datant de l'époque médiévale. L'idée de ce projet était aussi de moderniser le lieu en utilisant des détails qui inscrivent la maison dans le présent, à l'instar de l'apport de pierre obtenue sur le site et travaillée par des artisans locaux. L'étang est aménagé en objet décoratif, et le style industriel initial revêt de forts accents minimalistes. L'ensemble instaure un dialogue intéressant, né de la relation ininterrompue avec son passé historique.

Diese zu einem Landhaus umgestaltete alte Mühle im Cañon Padley steht auf einem Sandsteinhügel, dessen Farben von Graubraun bis Rosa reichen. Bei dem Umbau sollten vor allem zwei Elemente erhalten bleiben: die Wände aus grobem Sandstein, die das Gebäude mit der Umgebung verschmelzen lassen, und das Schieferdach, das noch aus dem Mittelalter stammt. Gleichzeitig sollte bei der Planung durch den Einsatz zeitgenössischer Elemente eine Modernisierung stattfinden. Dazu fügte man neue Steine hinzu, die aus der gleichen Gegend stammen und von örtlichen Handwerkern bearbeitet wurden. Den Teich gestalteten die Planer als einen Ort der Meditation und der lokale industrielle Stil wurde durch eine ausgeprägt minimalistische Dekoration unterstrichen. Das Gebäude scheint auf eine faszinierende Weise in einem ständigen Dialog mit seiner Geschichte zu stehen.

The mill stands on a hill of coarse sandstone, also known as millstone grit.

Le terrain de la colline où est situé le moulin est composé de grès à l'aspect granuleux, également appelé pierre de moulin.

Das Gelände, auf dem die Mühle steht, besteht aus grobem Sandstein, der auch als Mühlenstein bezeichnet wird.

The architects have fitted an additional steel girder to support the weight of the arched beams on the first floor.

Les architectes ont installé une poutre d'acier supplémentaire pour soutenir le poids des poutres courbes en bois du premier étage.

Die Architekten haben einen zusätzlichen Stahlträger eingebaut, um das Gewicht der verbogenen Holzbalken im ersten Stock zu stützen.

Timber Residence
Résidence en bois
Holzhaus

Wood, one of the most frequently employed building materials in Australian construction workowing to its great resistance, was chosen to make the structure of this project; in this particular case, the wood was recycled from old buildings. This construction is integrated into a rural setting typical of the eastern coastal region, based on a simple U-shaped layout enclosing a courtyard, which is a focus for the morning sunlight. As the local climate encourages inhabitants to spend more time outdoors than inside, it was decided to reinforce this connection with the exterior by giving every room an outside space with views of the sea. The guest bedrooms —designed as suites — are situated on the ground floor, whilst the upper floor contains the master bedroom, a small living room, a dressing room, a bathroom and a terrace.

Le bois, un des matériaux les plus utilisés en Australie dans le domaine de la construction, pour sa très grande résistance, est l'élément qui a été sélectionné pour réaliser la structure de ce projet : un bois dont la particularité est d'être recyclé à partir d'anciens bâtiments. Cet édifice est immergé dans l'environnement champêtre caractéristique de la région de la côte, selon un plan qui s'articule suivant un schéma simple en forme de U, tournant autour d'un patio qui apprivoise la lumière naturelle du matin. Le climat de cette zone permettant aux résidents de passer plus de temps à l'extérieur qu'à l'intérieur de la maison, les architectes ont décidé de maximaliser l'union avec l'environnement, en dotant chaque chambre d'un espace extérieur donnant sur la mer. Les chambres d'amis – sous forme de suite –, sont situées au rez-de-chaussée, tandis que l'étage supérieur abrite la chambre à coucher des propriétaires, un petit salon, un dressing, une salle de bains et une terrasse.

Für die Struktur dieses Hauses wählte man das Baumaterial Holz, das in Australien aufgrund seiner großen Widerstandsfähigkeit eine sehr wichtige Rolle spielt. In diesem Fall handelt es sich um recyceltes Holz, das aus alten Gebäuden stammt. Das Haus steht in einer typischen wilden Landschaft an der Ostküste. Es ist in einer einfachen U-Form angelegt und umgibt einen Hof, in den morgens die Sonne scheint. Aufgrund des milden Klimas halten sich die Bewohner des Hauses mehr draußen als drinnen auf. Deshalb wurde bei der Planung die Verbindung zur Umgebung verstärkt und jedes Zimmer hat einen Außenbereich mit Blick auf das Meer. Die Gästezimmer sind in Form von Suiten gestaltet und liegen im Erdgeschoss. Im Obergeschoss befinden sich das Schlafzimmer, ein kleines Wohnzimmer, ein Ankleidezimmer, ein Bad und eine Terrasse.

› **Ground floor** Rez-de-chaussée Erdgeschoss

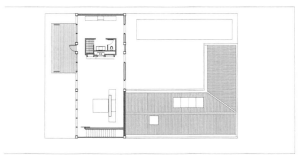

› **First floor** Premier étage Erstes Obergeschoss

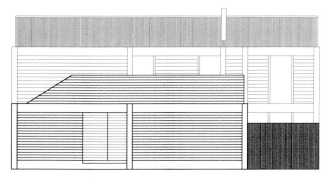

› South elevation Élévation sud Südlicher Aufriss

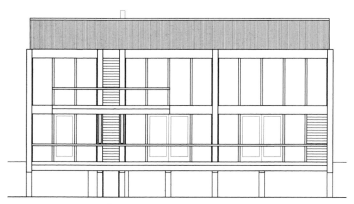

› North elevation Élévation nord Nördlicher Aufriss

The bedroom, with its own private terrace and French windows, enjoys magnificent views of the ocean.

La chambre à coucher, agrémentée d'une terrasse privée et d'amples fenêtres du sol au plafond, offre des vues magnifiques sur l'océan.

Das Schlafzimmer hat eine eigene Terrasse und Fenster vom Boden bis zur Decke, so dass man einen wundervollen Blick auf das Meer hat.

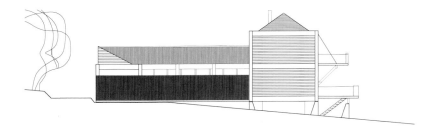

› West elevation Élévation ouest Westlicher Aufriss

› East elevation Élévation est Östlicher Aufriss

Residence in Normandy

Résidence en Normandie

Haus in der Normandie

A simple masía, or traditional Catalan farmhouse, has been converted into a vacation home in the country. The derelict state of the old stone house made it necessary to restore the structure, and to put in a new kitchen and bathroom. The new part of the house draws on traditional forms to establish clear associations with the past and create a restful atmosphere. As well as the purely functional aspects, the convertion sought to combine distinct environments: a transition from the old construction to the new, imbued with both nostalgia and originality. Two independent extensions to the original building also reflect this approach, in which space, light, materials and colors provide the occupants with a wide range of different sensations.

Ce projet a permis de convertir une simple ferme isolée en une maison de campagne pour les vacances. La demeure, construite en pierres de carrière, étant en ruine, la conception a visé essentiellement la reconstruction de la structure et l'installation d'une cuisine et d'une salle de bains. La nouvelle partie de la résidence arbore des lignes et des formes authentiques engendrant des associations d'idées et images claires et recréant une atmosphère reposante. A la transformation d'ordre purement fonctionnel, s'ajoute la création d'un ensemble de divers univers : une transition entre l'ancien et le nouvel édifice, empreinte à la fois de nostalgie et d'originalité. Le projet propose de créer deux agrandissements indépendants, où l'espace, la lumière, les matériaux et les couleurs présentent diverses solutions procurant aux occupants des lieux un large éventail de sensations.

Bei diesem Renovierungsprojekt wurde ein allein stehendes Landhaus in ein Ferienhaus umgebaut. Das Gebäude besteht aus Natursteinen aus einem Steinbruch. Es war baufällig, so dass man zunächst die Struktur wieder aufbauen und dann eine Küche und ein Bad schaffen musste. Im neuen Teil des Hauses wurden sehr klare Formen und Linien geschaffen, durch die eine entspannte und ruhige Atmosphäre entstand. Zusätzlich zu dem rein funktionellen Umbau wurden auch verschiedene Umgebungen miteinander kombiniert, so dass ein Übergang zwischen dem alten und dem neuen Gebäude entstand, der gleichzeitig nostalgisch und außergewöhnlich wirkt. Dabei wurden auch zwei voneinander unabhängige Bereiche geschaffen, in denen der Raum, das Licht, die Materialien und die Farben verschiedene Alternativen anbieten, so dass sehr vielseitige und verschiedene Sinneseindrücke für die Bewohner hervorgerufen werden.

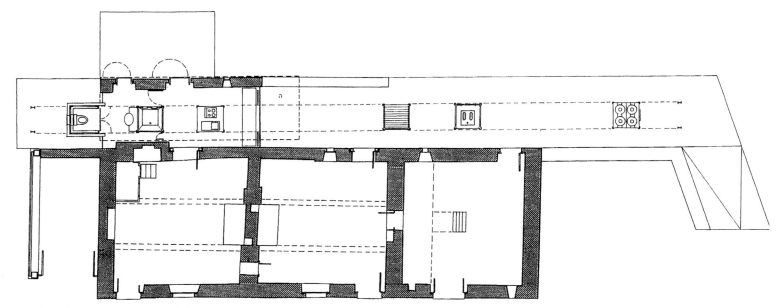

› Ground floor   Rez-de-chaussée   Erdgeschoss

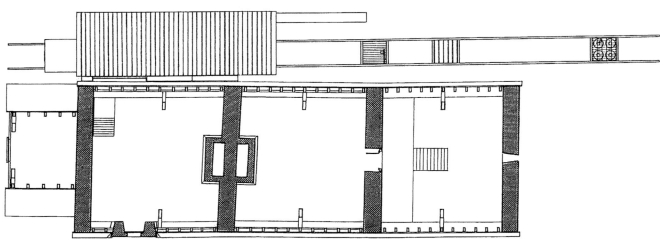

› First floor   Premier étage   Erstes Obergeschoss

308

The new building has used many features from the pre-existing structure to great advantage.

Le nouvel édifice a été construit en utilisant, pour l'essentiel, la structure antérieure.

Bei der Konstruktion des neuen Gebäudes benutzte man einen großen Teil der bereits existierenden Struktur.

Gold Lane

The combination of environmentally friendly solutions, affordable prices and a structure permitting various lifestyles was the key factor in this development, which transformed an unsafe area surrounding forty-five abandoned garages into a residential complex. The most striking feature is the rooftops covered with short grass, easy to maintain and a source of superb insulation. Since they are accessible, these roofs also serve as terraces, above all for the houses at the ends of the streets, which have a greater surface area. Energy-saving solutions are also to be found inside, in the form of openings permitting the entrance of abundant sunlight, good insulation materials and condensation heaters. This is an example of how low-budget architecture can produce pleasant, environmentally respectful living space, open to new ideas.

L'association de solutions écologiques, de coûts réduits et d'une structure s'adaptant à divers modes de vie est la clé de voûte de ce projet, qui a transformé une zone peu sécurisée, configurée autour de quarante cinq garages abandonnés, en un environnement habitable. La solution la plus étonnante consiste à réaliser des toitures recouvertes de gazon, d'entretien facile, offrant de surcroît une isolation incomparable. Dotées de zone d'accès, ces toitures se convertissent en terrasses praticables, surtout dans le cas des habitations situées aux extrémités des rues, disposant d'une plus grande superficie. Les intérieurs, en quête de solutions pour économiser l'énergie, sont dotés d'ouvertures permettant l'entrée d'une abondante lumière naturelle, de chaudières de condensation et de bons isolants thermiques. C'est un exemple d'architecture montrant que même avec un budget serré, il est possible de créer un lieu de vie agréable, tout en respectant l'environnement, ouvert à toute conception nouvelle.

Die Kombination von ökologischen und kostengünstigen Lösungen und eine Struktur, die man an verschiedene Lebensweisen anpassen kann, war der wichtigste Aspekt bei der Planung dieser Anlage. Ein nicht sehr sicheres Gelände, auf dem sich ungefähr fünfundvierzig verlassene Garagen befanden, wurde zu einer bewohnbaren Zone umgestaltet. Die auffälligsten Elemente, die entstanden, sind die Dächer, auf denen kurzgeschnittenes Gras wächst, das pflegeleicht ist und für gute Isolierung sorgt. Da man diese Dächer betreten kann, werden sie zu Gärten, vor allem in den Häusern am Ende der Straßen, die ein größeres Dach besitzen. Auch im Inneren suchte man nach energiesparenden Lösungen wie Fenster, die reichlich Tageslicht in die Räume lassen, Kondensationskessel und eine gute Wärmeisolierung. Es handelt sich um ein ausgezeichnetes Beispiel für eine Architektur, bei der man für wenig Geld eine komfortable Wohnumgebung geschaffen hat, die respektvoll mit der Umwelt umgeht und offen für jede Veränderung ist.

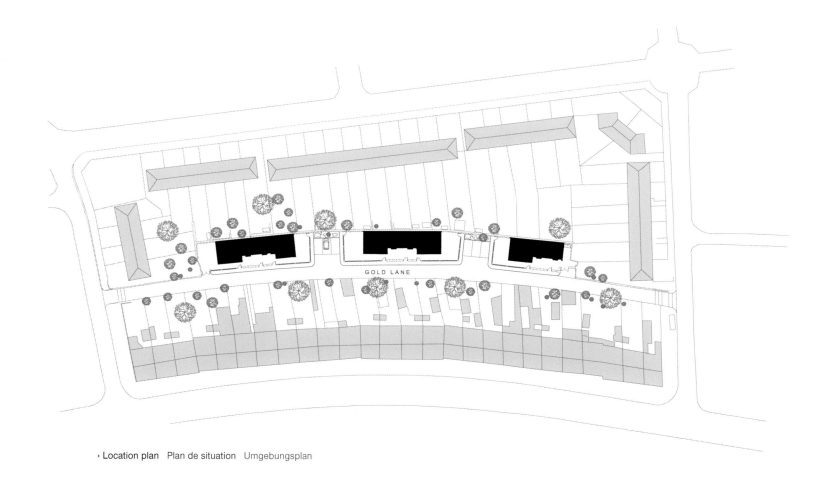

GOLD LANE

› Location plan   Plan de situation   Umgebungsplan

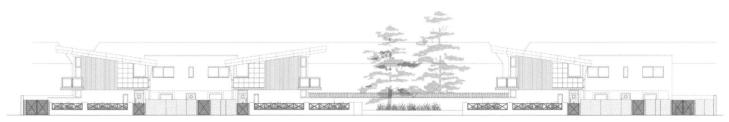

› Elevation Élévation Aufriss

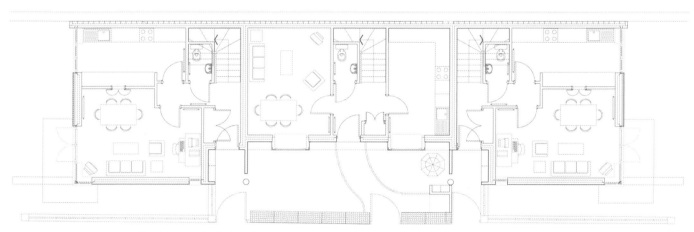

› Ground floor Rez-de-chaussée Erdgeschoss

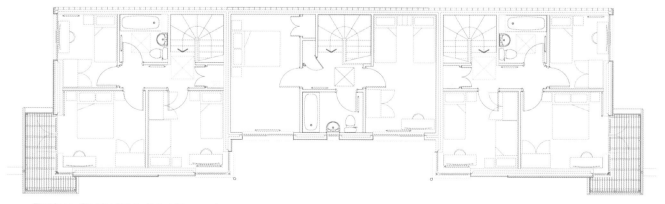

› First floor Premier étage Erstes Obergeschoss

A set of old garages has been transformed into a model residential complex.

La réhabilitation d'anciens garages les a transformés en un complexe résidentiel modèle.

Zwei ehemalige Garagen wurden zu einem Wohnkomplex mit Modellcharakter umgebaut.

House in Tiana

Maison à Tiana

Haus in Tiana

The transformation of this old farmhouse into a home involved major changes in the spatial distribution. The old building had a storage area on the lower floor and two upper stories that were poorly lit, owing to the narrow windows and layout typical of the period. The windows of the front and rear façades have been left untouched, but the side walls, facing east and west, have been pierced with openings running along their entire length. The new layout has made the rooms bigger, while ensuring that they all open on to the exterior. However, the most innovative feature of this project is the addition of an expansive terrace on the first floor, whose slender outlines and metal construction, reminiscent of a garden trellis, serve as a porch for the ground floor.

La transformation de cette ancienne ferme agricole en une habitation a profondément modifié la distribution de l'espace. L'ancienne demeure disposait d'un rez-de-chaussée, accueillant un entrepôt, et de deux niveaux supérieurs très peu éclairés, dû à l'organisation des chambres et à l'étroitesse des fenêtres, comme cela se faisait autrefois. Sur les façades antérieure et postérieure, les fenêtres ont été conservées telles qu'elles étaient, mais sur les façades latérales – orientées sur l'axe est-ouest – ont été pratiquées des ouvertures qui occupent toute la longueur. La nouvelle distribution intérieure permet que les chambres soient plus grandes et donnent toujours sur l'extérieur. Cependant, l'élément le plus innovateur de ce projet, est la création d'une terrasse extrêmement large au niveau du premier étage. Sa structure, réalisée en fins profils métallisés, imprègne l'ensemble de légèreté et fait office de porche au rez-de-chaussée, rappelant les fines structures pour plantes grimpantes et séchoirs des maisons rurales.

Um diesen ehemaligen Bauernhof in ein Wohnhaus umzubauen, musste man die Raumaufteilung radikal verändern. In dem einstigen Hof befand sich im Erdgeschoss ein Lager und die beiden oberen Stockwerke waren aufgrund der Raumaufteilung und der schmalen, für alte Häuser typischen Fenster sehr dunkel. An den Hauptfassaden wurden die Fenster so erhalten wie sie einst waren; an den nach Osten und Westen hin ausgerichteten Seitenwänden hingegen wurden Fenster eingesetzt, die die gesamte Länge des Gebäudes einnehmen. Durch die neue Raumaufteilung sind die Räume grösser und zeigen alle nach aussen. Das innovativste Gestaltungselement jedoch ist eine neue, große Terrasse im ersten Stockwerk mit einer Struktur aus feinen Metallprofilen, die sie sehr leicht wirken lässt. Sie dient gleichzeitig als Vorhalle für das Erdgeschoss und erinnert an die feinen Strukturen der Schlingpflanzen und Trockenplätze der Landhäuser.

There used to be a warehouse on the ground floor of the old building, while the living quarters were set in the two upper levels.

Le rez-de-chaussée de l'ancien édifice abritait un entrepôt. L'habitation occupait seulement les deux étages supérieurs.

Im Erdgeschoss des bereits existierenden Gebäudes gab es ein Lager, so dass der Wohnbereich sich nur über die beiden oberen Geschosse erstreckte.

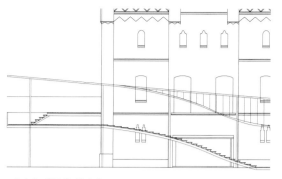

› Detail   Détail   Detail

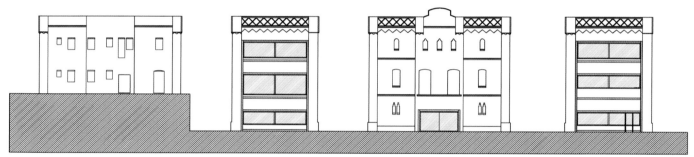

› Elevations   Élévations   Aufrisse

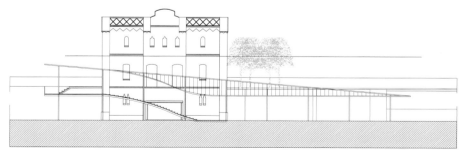

› Elevation   Élévation   Aufriss

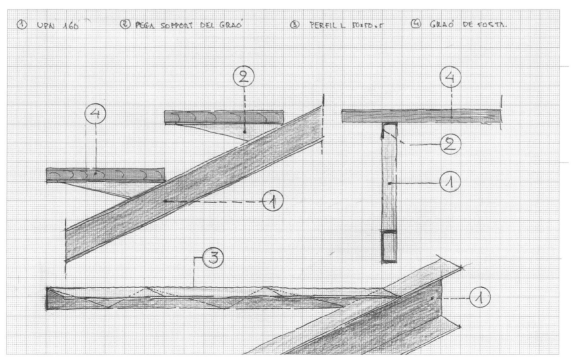

① UPN 160   ② PEGA SOPPORT DEL GRAÓ   ③ PERFIL L 50×50.5   ④ GRAÓ DE FOSTA.

› Stairway construction detail   Détail de construction de l'escalier   Konstruktionsdetail des Treppenhauses

The new interior layout has created into larger rooms, all of which look out onto the exterior.

La nouvelle distribution intérieure a agrandi les pièces qui donnent toutes sur l'extérieur.

Durch die neue Raumaufteilung wurden alle Zimmer größer und liegen zur Fassade.

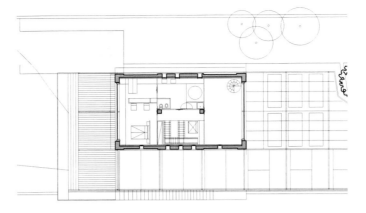

› **Ground floor** Rez-de-chaussée Erdgeschoss

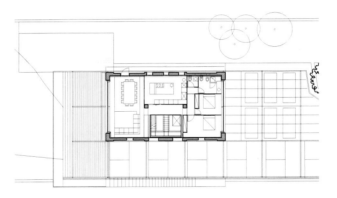

› **First floor** Premier étage Erstes Obergeschoss

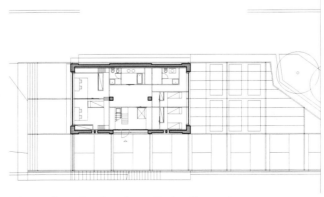

› **Second floor** Deuxième étage Zweites Obergeschoss

One of the most innovative aspects of this project is the light, modern kitchen, endowed with a metal structure.

La cuisine, un des éléments les plus innovateurs de ce projet, est dotée d'une structure métallique, lui conférant légèreté et modernisme.

Eines der innovativsten Elemente dieser Raumgestaltung ist die Küche, deren Struktur aus Metall sie leicht und modern wirken lässt.

Villa Råman

An old country schoolhouse featuring two classrooms and a gym on the first floor was converted into a spacious, uncluttered home. Each of the different areas in the original building was stripped of all obstacles to achieve maximum freedom of circulation. The austere interior, with its minimalist lines and neutral white finishes, conveys an almost monastic starkness. The main bedroom and the guest room are arranged on the ground floor, with the kitchen, dining room and workroom upstairs, inside the old classroom walls. Sliding glass doors separate the dining room from the workroom, providing privacy but letting in the daylight. Pine floorboards were laid throughout most of the house, except in the bathroom, where cool clay tiles were used.

Une ancienne école rurale, dotée de deux salles de classe et d'un gymnase à l'étage supérieur, a été transformée en une demeure très simple et spacieuse. Les différentes zones de l'édifice original se sont épurées laissant place à un intérieur dépourvu d'objets obstruant le passage, propice à la mobilité. Fort de ses lignes minimalistes et presque entièrement paré de la neutralité du blanc, l'intérieur est caractérisé par une austérité quasi monacale. Au rez-de-chaussée se trouvent la chambre des propriétaires et la chambre d'amis, alors que l'étage supérieur héberge – entre les murs de ce que furent les anciennes classes d'école – la cuisine, la salle à manger et l'office. Ces deux dernières zones sont séparées par des portes coulissantes en verre, qui préservent l'intimité tout en laissant passer la lumière naturelle. Le sol de la demeure est en grande partie en bois de pin, à l'exception de la zone de la salle de bains, où l'argile du carrelage imprègne la pièce de fraîcheur.

Eine alte Landschule, die zwei Klassenräume und einen Sportsaal im Obergeschoss besaß, wurde zu einer einfachen und geräumigen Wohnung umgebaut. Die verschiedenen Bereiche des Originalgebäudes wurden geleert, um Innenräume zu schaffen, in denen sich keinerlei Objekte befinden, die die Zirkulation und die Mobilität behindern. Das Innere ist in minimalistischen Linien und fast vollständig in der Farbe Weiß gehalten, so dass es relativ nüchtern, nahezu klösterlich wirkt. Im Erdgeschoss befinden sich das Schlafzimmer und das Gästezimmer, und im Obergeschoss zwischen den Wänden, die einst die alten Schulräume begrenzten, die Küche, das Speisezimmer und das Büro. Die beiden letztgenannten Bereiche werden durch gläserne Schiebetüren voneinander getrennt. Diese Türen sorgen für die notwendige Privatsphäre, lassen aber das Tageslicht durch. Der Boden der Wohnung besteht zum größten Teil aus Kiefernholz. Nur im Bad sorgen Tonfliesen für eine frische Atmosphäre.

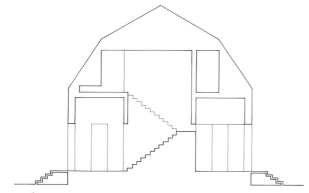

› Elevation Élévation Aufriss

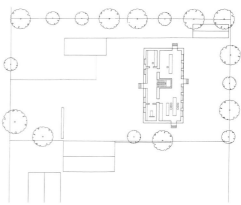

› Location plan Plan de situation Umgebungsplan

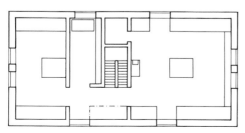

› Plan Plan Grundriss

The large windows allow the entire house to be in contact with its surroundings and enjoy the changes in sunlight over the course of the day.

Les amples fenêtres permettent à l'ensemble de la maison d'être en contact avec l'environnement et de bénéficier des changements de lumière au fil de la journée.

Die großen Fenster verbinden das gesamte Haus mit der Umgebung, und man kann in allen Räumen die Veränderungen des Lichts im Tagesverlauf miterleben.

A fireplace serves for cooking, as well as providing heating for several rooms.

La cheminée sert à faire la cuisine et à chauffer les diverses salles.

Der Kamin dient zum Kochen und zum Heizen der verschiedenen Räume.

In the bathroom, pale colors and natural materials such as wood harmonize with the rest of the space.

Des couleurs claires et des matériaux neutres s'affichent dans la salle de bains, comme le bois, en harmonie avec le reste de l'espace.

Im Bad wurden helle Farben und natürliche Materialien wie Holz verwendet, die mit den übrigen Räumen harmonieren.

Old Stable

Ancienne étable

Ein ehemaliger Stall

The structure of this house detaches itself from the superficial appearance of an inert architecture and adopts the form of a living organism that grows and turns greener with rain, like a gigantic geometric plant that camouflages the house behind its suit of evergreen leaves. Bathed in the heat of the sunshine, oxygenated by the breath of Nature, and enhanced by the nuanced lyricism of pink and red flowers, the interior of the house is engulfed by the calm of a slowly prepared infusion of medicinal herbs gathered in some enchanted forest. Delicacy, details, and moments emanating from objects give soul to the inanimate body that day after day bears witness to the domestic routine. Nature's splendor impregnates the interior and exterior of the house, illuminating its warm and peaceful heart at nightfall.

La structure de cette habitation s'écarte de l'apparence superficielle d'une architecture inerte et se présente comme un organisme vivant, qui croit et reverdit avec la pluie, à l'instar d'une gigantesque plante géométrique qui camoufle derrière son costume de feuilles perpétuelles le corps réduit de la maison. Baignée de la chaleur issue de la lumière naturelle, oxygénée par la respiration de la nature et parée des nuances lyriques tout en rose et rouge des fleurs, l'habitation est enveloppée de la douceur d'une infusion d'herbes médicinales recueillies dans un bois enchanté. Délicatesse, détails et instants qui émanent d'objets et donnent une âme au corps inanimé effectuant, jour après jour, le quotidien familial. L'exubérance de la nature imprègne l'intérieur et l'extérieur de la maison de vie tout en illuminant son coeur paisible et chaleureux à la tombée de la nuit.

Die Struktur dieser Wohnung leitet sich von dem oberflächlich gesehenen Erscheinungsbild einer leblosen Architektur ab; sie wurde wie ein lebendiger Organismus gestaltet, der wächst und mit dem Regen grün wird. Eine Art gigantische geometrische Pflanze, hinter deren immergrünen Blättern der begrenzte Körper des Hauses verborgen ist. Tageslicht umgibt das Haus mit Wärme, der Atem der Natur belüftet es und das Rosa und Rot der Blumen verleihen ihm einen lyrischen Charakter. Das Haus wirkt, als ob es von der Ruhe eines Tees aus Heilkräutern umgeben ist, die in einem verzauberten Wald gesammelt wurden. Der unbelebte Körper, der jeden Tag das alltägliche Leben bezeugt, wird von Zartheit, kleinen Einzelheiten und Momenten, die von den Objekten ausströmen, beseelt. Die Zurschaustellung der Natur imprägniert das Leben im Inneren und Äußeren des Hauses und beleuchtet das friedliche und warme Herz dieses Gebäudes, wenn die Nacht beginnt.

The combination of white-painted walls and wooden floors conjures up a natural, minimalist feeling.

L'association de murs peints en blanc et de sols en bois forge une ambiance naturelle et minimaliste.

Das Zusammenspiel der weissgestrichenen Wände mit dem Holzboden lässt ein natürliches und minimalistisches Gefühl entstehen.

Temple of Love
Temple de l'amour
Tempel der Liebe

The idea to restore this unusual building in a magnificent natural setting arose from the accidental discovery of an arched room located inside an old railroad building destroyed during the war. At first, it was only possible to gain entry through the top, via a small trapdoor. So, another opening was inserted at a lower level in order to permit access, allow in sunlight and provide views of the river. In the upper level, a very unusual space has been designed, offering direct contact with nature and minimal visual impact. Owing to the characteristics of the location, it was decided to lay the roof on reinforced glass panels, thereby supplying 360° panoramic views. Outside, a pale green, tinted-glass bench, with supports reminiscent of railroad tracks, reflects the canopy of trees and part of the building, in the same way as of a pond.

L'idée de récupérer cette construction originale et son superbe environnement naturel, est née de la découverte accidentelle d'une salle voûtée située à l'intérieur d'un ancien pilier massif de chemin de fer détruit pendant la guerre. A l'origine, l'accès ne se faisait que par le haut, grâce à une petite trappe. Il a donc fallu pratiquer une ouverture dans la zone inférieure pour y accéder, laisser passer la lumière naturelle et profiter des vues sur le fleuve. La partie supérieure, abrite une pièce très particulière, en contact direct avec la nature, dont l'impact visuel est minime. Les caractéristiques du lieu sont déterminantes dans la conception d'une toiture appuyée sur des panneaux de verre laminé, visant à créer une vue panoramique de trois cent soixante degrés. A l'extérieur, un banc en verre légèrement teinté de vert, dont les supports ne sont pas sans rappeler les rails de chemin de fer, reflète, tel un étang, la voûte arborée et une partie de l'édifice.

Die Idee, diese Konstruktion wieder herzustellen und die wundervolle umgebende Natur zu erhalten, entstand, als man durch Zufall einen Saal mit einem Gewölbe in einem alten Eisenbahndepot entdeckte, das während des Krieges zerstört worden war. Zunächst konnte man diesen Raum nur vom Obergeschoss aus durch eine kleine Klappe erreichen. Deshalb schuf man unten eine Öffnung, um Licht hinein zu lassen und den Blick auf den Fluss freizugeben. Im Obergeschoss entwarfen die Planer eine sehr eigentümliche Wohnung, die in direktem Kontakt mit der Natur steht und in der Landschaft nur minimal wahrgenommen wird. Aufgrund der Charakteristika der Umgebung entwarf man ein Dach, das sich auf Paneele aus gewalztem Glas stützt und durch das man einen Panoramablick rundum genießt. Draußen reflektiert eine Glasbank, die leicht grün getönt ist und deren Stützen an Eisenbahnschienen erinnern, fast wie ein Gartenteich die Baumkuppeln und einen Teil des Gebäudes.

› Cross section Section transversale Querschnitt

› Front elevation Élévation frontale Vorderansicht

› Longitudinal section Section longitudinale Längsschnitt

› Side elevation Élévation latérale Seitenansicht

348

This construction's delicate, fragile qualities are a perfect match for the surrounding landscape.

La fragilité et la beauté de ce corps se moulent parfaitement dans le paysage environnant.

Dieser Körper mit seiner Zerbrechlichkeit und Schönheit schmiegt sich perfekt in die umgebende Landschaft ein.

The abundance of glass has enabled the romanticism and beauty of the ruins to survive unblemished.

L'abondance du verre permet de respecter le romantisme et la beauté des ruines.

Indem man viel Glas verwendete, blieben das romantische Aussehen und die Schönheit der Ruinen erhalten.

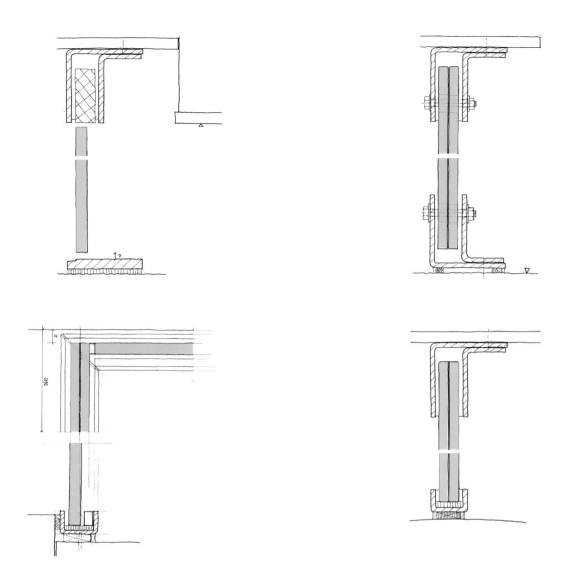

› Glass structure details   Détails structure en verre   Details der Glasstruktur

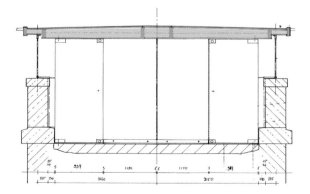

› Section detail   Détail section   Schnittdetail

An opening in the base allows the natural light to penetrate inside, while also providing the bedroom and the living room with superb views of the river.

Une ouverture dans la zone inférieure permet l'accès de la lumière et de bénéficier des vues sur le fleuve, depuis la chambre à coucher et le salon.

Eine Öffnung im unteren Bereich lässt Licht ein und gestattet den Blick zum Fluss, den man vom Wohn- und Schlafzimmer aus genießen kann.

House in Raasdorf

Maison à Raasdorf

Haus in Raasdorf

This farmhouse needed a restoration that catered to the owner's two occupations: farming and philology. This premise called for a site adapted to various agricultural activities but also equipped with a library. A first floor extension with a modern design was conceived to accommodate the library, while reflecting the rural characteristics of the original structure. Thus, the brickwork base that once contained the stables was retained and converted into living quarters: the higher sections of the outer walls, in danger of collapse, were replaced by a smooth, reflective aluminum façade. The outward contrast draws attention to the dual function of the new building, whilst also marrying traditional architecture with contemporary style.

Cette maison d'agriculteur a été essentiellement restaurée en fonction du désir du propriétaire de disposer d'un espace qui puisse conjuguer ses deux occupations, l'agriculture et la philologie : un lieu où il puisse développer plusieurs activités agricoles et qui dispose également d'une bibliothèque. Le projet concerne donc l'agrandissement du premier étage selon un tracé aux lignes modernes – abritant la bibliothèque – tout en conservant le caractère rural qui se dégage de la structure originale. Le socle en briques qui, autrefois, accueillait l'étable, a été conservé pour convertir ce volume en espace habitable. La partie supérieure de la façade, dont certaines zones risquaient de s'écrouler, a été remplacée par une façade d'aluminium lisse et réfléchissante. Le contraste extérieur, indication visuelle relevant la double fonctionnalité de la construction, est en même temps une intervention architecturale qui souligne le respect mutuel entre l'architecture traditionnelle et contemporaine.

Dieses Bauernhaus sollte so renoviert werden, dass dem Eigentümer zwei Möglichkeiten offen stehen, die seinen Tätigkeiten entsprechen; er widmet sich der Landwirtschaft und der Philologie. In diesem Haus wollte er sowohl den verschiedenen landwirtschaftlichen Tätigkeiten nachgehen als auch über eine großzügige Bibliothek verfügen. Im ersten Stock wurde eine moderne Wohnumgebung geschaffen, in der sich diese Bibliothek befindet und die gleichzeitig auch den ländlichen Charakter des Hauses bewahrt. So gestaltete man den Ziegelsteinbau, in dem sich einst der Stall befand, zu einem Wohnraum um. Der obere Teil der Fassade, der sich in einem sehr schlechten Zustand befand, wurde durch eine glatte und reflektierende Aluminiumfassade ersetzt. Dieser Kontrast an der Fassade dient gleichzeitig als visuelle Information über die doppelte Funktion des Gebäudes. Dennoch wurde bei diesem baulichen Eingriff sowohl die traditionelle als auch die zeitgenössische Architektur streng respektiert.

The architects' main objective was to satisfy the owners' needs without creating an artificial effect or disrupting the surrounding landscape.

L'objectif principal des architectes était d'atteindre un résultat satisfaisant, selon les besoins des propriétaires, qui ne soit ni artificiel, ni imposé au paysage alentour.

Das Hauptziel der Architekten war die Befriedigung der Kundenwünsche, ohne dabei etwas Künstliches zu schaffen oder die Landschaft zu vereiteln.

Openings in the walls and roof allow plenty of natural light to reach the interior.

Les ouvertures dans les murs et le toit laissent la lumière naturelle pénétrer l'intérieur de l'habitation.

Die Öffnungen in den Wänden und im Dach lassen das Tageslicht in die Räume fallen.

The interior is embellished with pale wood finishing, which reflects the natural daylight.

L'intérieur affiche des finitions en bois clair, reflétant ainsi la lumière naturelle.

Im Inneren herrschen Flächen aus hellem Holz vor, die das Tageslicht reflektieren.

The modern bathroom contrasts with the overall structure, engaging in a fluent dialogue with traditional architecture.

La salle de bains, de style contemporain, contraste avec la structure qui l'accueille, instaurant un dialogue constant avec l'architecture traditionnelle.

Das modern gestaltete Bad steht im Gegensatz zu der Struktur, in der es sich befindet, und lässt so einen ständigen Dialog mit der traditionellen Architektur entstehen.

Teng Kunyen Studio
Studio Teng Kunyen
Studio von Teng Kunyen

When Teng Kunyen chose these old industrial premises on the banks of the Suzhou River in 1997 to set up his own architectural studio, the area was in a sorry state. The recovery of Shanghai's urban fabric has exceeded even this architect's own expectations, however, and both sides of the river have experienced a dizzying renovation. The conversion preserved the old structure, with its wood and steel beams. The insertion of skylights allows light to flow into the interior and the predominance of white creates a luminous and welcoming atmosphere. The old structure now comprises a bookstore on the ground floor and two architectural studios on the upper levels.

Lorsqu'en 1997 Teng Kunyen choisit ces vieux bâtiments industriels, installés sur les berges de la Suzhou River, pour construire son bureau d'architecture, la zone se trouvait alors dans un état déplorable. La restauration de l'usine urbaine de Shanghai a dépassé les espérances de cet architecte, et les deux côtés de la rivière ont été rénovés de manière éblouissante. La restauration a préservé les poutres de bois et d'acier de l'ancienne structure. L'insertion de puits de lumière permet à la lumière d'inonder l'intérieur. La prédominance du blanc crée une atmosphère lumineuse et accueillante. L'ancien bâtiment restauré abrite désormais une librairie au rez-de-chaussée et deux studios d'architecture aux niveaux supérieurs.

Als Teng Kunyen im Jahr 1997 dieses alte Industriegelände am Ufer des Flusses Suzhou auswählte, um hier sein eigenes Architekturstudio zu errichten, befand sich das Gelände in einem sehr schlechten Zustand. Die Wiederbelebung der Stadtstruktur in diesem Viertel von Shanghai hat sogar die Erwartungen des Architekten selbst übertroffen, denn auf beiden Seiten des Flusses hat mit schwindelerregender Geschwindigkeit eine Stadterneuerung stattgefunden. Bei dem Umbau blieb die alte Struktur mit ihren Holzbalken und Stahlträgern erhalten. Es wurden Dachfenster eingebaut, um mehr Tageslicht in die Räume zu lassen, und es dominiert die Farbe Weiß, so dass die Atmosphäre sehr einladend und hell ist. Die alte Struktur enthält heute einen Buchladen im Erdgeschoss und zwei Architekturstudios in den oberen Stockwerken.

Gallery Residence
Habitation pinacothèque
Haus und Pinakothek

What were once the headquarters of an electric cable manufacturers is now a home, catering to the wishes of its owners by housing their growing collection of paintings and sculptures without impinging on the privacy of the private living area. From a structural point of view, this new volume is completely independent from the main block of the former industrial building. The classical iron and concrete structure is surrounded by a patio containing an assortment of building materials and industrial artefacts, the fruit of two generations of urban regeneration that made up most of the elements used to create the new space. This distinctive and complex construction is based on a series of wave-shaped pieces resting on six different base-points, which form a simple structural framework surrounding the building.

Ce qui fut un jour le siège d'une compagnie de fabrication de câbles électriques, est aujourd'hui une habitation conçue en fonction des voeux des propriétaires, à savoir accueillir leur collection grandissante de peintures et de sculptures sans compromettre l'intimité de l'espace réservé au foyer. D'un point de vue structurel, ce nouveau volume est entièrement indépendant du périmètre de l'installation industrielle préexistante. La structure classique d'acier et de béton brut est ici entourée d'un patio contenant toute une collection de matériaux de construction et d'engins industriels, fruit de deux générations de travail et rénovation urbaine. Elle est utilisée, en grande partie, pour construire le nouvel espace. Cette construction singulière et complexe s'appuie sur un système de cintres en forme de vague surgissant d'un cadre structurel simple qui ceint l'édifice en se reposant sur six points différents.

Wo sich einst eine Fabrik befand, die Elektrokabel produzierte, befindet sich jetzt eine Wohnung, in der die Eigentümer ihre ständig wachsende Sammlung an Gemälden und Skulpturen unterbringen wollten, ohne dabei an Privatsphäre zu verlieren. Unter strukturellen Gesichtspunkten ist dieses neue Gebäude vollkommen unabhängig von dem Körper der bereits existierenden, industriellen Bebauung. Die klassische Struktur aus nacktem Stahl und Beton ist in diesem Fall von einem Hof umgeben, in dem sich eine umfassende Sammlung von Baumaterialien und industriellen Vorrichtungen befindet, die sich über zwei Generationen von Arbeit und Stadterneuerung angesammelt haben, und zu einem großen Teil auch aus der Errichtung des neuen Gebäudes stammen. Dieses einzigartige und komplexe Gebäude stützt sich auf ein System von wellenförmigen Trägern, die einem einfachen Strukturrahmen entspringen, der den Kern des Gebäudes umgibt und auf sechs verschiedenen Punkten ruht.

The new volume is fully independent of the pre-existing industrial premises.

Le nouveau volume est complètement indépendant de l'installation industrielle préexistante.

Der neue Gebäudeteil ist vollkommen unabhängig von der bereits existierenden industriellen Struktur.

The tall ceilings, which enhance the great sense of spaciousness, are a legacy from the structure's industrial past.

La hauteur des toits accentue la profonde sensation d'espace, rappelant le passé industriel de la structure.

Die hohen Decken, die an die industrielle Vergangenheit des Gebäudes erinnern, lassen einen Eindruck von Geräumigkeit entstehen.

Lowering the ceilings has given the living and night-time areas a greater degree of privacy.

Diminuer la hauteur des toits, permet d'accentuer le caractère privé des zones de vie et des zones de nuit.

Die Wohnbereiche und die Zonen für die Nacht wurden intimer und mit mehr Privatsphäre gestaltet, indem man die Decken etwas abhängte.

Photo Credits   Crédits photographiques   Fotonachweis